More pra

"This book will serve anyoi
tion to reading the parables.
marginal notes and signs, marking where my mind absorbed new information or where I suddenly (and unexpectedly) recognized various aspects of my own life at that reading moment. I have no doubt others will appreciate their own version of this experience."

—Jaime Clark-Soles, Professor of New Testament,
Perkins School of Theology

"Greg Carey succeeds in avoiding the extremes of oversimplifying the parables or losing them in scholarly complexities. He brings this distinctive feature of Jesus' teaching alive in ways that challenge us to think beyond the commonplace to the extraordinary truths of the kingdom revealed in stories that begin in the commonplace but take us deeper into our own lives. Like the disciples, we may not fully understand but we are transformed in the process of thinking more deeply about the claims the kingdom makes on us."

—Bruce C. Birch, Dean Emeritus and Professor Emeritus
of Biblical Theology, Wesley Theological Seminary

"Greg Carey has produced a wonderful introduction to the off-key, strange, ambiguous, and often misunderstood stories Jesus told. Awash with scholarly insight, Carey leads ordinary readers past popular, often simplistic and tamed, readings of the parables to a deeper level of understanding—one that embraces the challenges posed by the parables for the church today."

—Peter Enns, author of *How the Bible Actually Works*

Stories Jesus Told

Stories Jesus Told

978-1-5018-8415-3
978-1-5018-8416-0 eBook

Stories Jesus Told DVD

978-1-5018-8417-7

Stories Jesus Told Leader Guide

978-1-5018-8424-5
978-1-5018-8425-2 eBook

GREG CAREY

STORIES

JESUS

TOLD

HOW TO READ
A PARABLE

Abingdon Press / Nashville

Stories Jesus Told

How to Read a Parable

Library of Congress Control Number: 2019942311

ISBN: 978-1-5018-8415-3

19 20 21 22 23 24 25 26 27 28 — 10 9 8 7 6 5 4 3 2 1
MANUFACTURED IN THE UNITED STATES OF AMERICA

In memory of Dr. Charles F. Melchert, an extraordinary teacher, mentor, and friend who modeled the value of wise questions and never settled for pat answers.

Contents

Introduction ix

1. Divine Inefficiencies 1

2. Funny Business 19

3. Weddings Gone Awry 35

4. Lawyers and Samaritans 49

5. Losing, Finding, Partying 67

6. A Reversal of Fortune 85

Afterword 101

Resources for Parable Interpretation 107

Notes 109

Introduction

Work your way through the Gospels, and it's hard to avoid the impression that Jesus is frequently misunderstood. Often the problem lies with the people who encounter Jesus: people can be just, well, obtuse, and Jesus' commitment to truth and grace can be far too much for us to take in. We may attribute some of the miscommunication to Jesus' enemies, who have no interest in understanding him correctly. We might expect that if anyone would come around and understand Jesus, it should be his disciples, but they suffer pretty much the same incomprehension as everyone else. The disciples often succeed spectacularly: they leave everything to follow Jesus, they often follow his directions to the letter, they even perform healings and exorcisms. But time and again, their failure to understand shows through.

On close inspection it seems the disconnect lies not just with the disciples and not just with Jesus' audiences but with Jesus himself. That is, Jesus chooses to communicate in indirect ways. In John's Gospel, he prefers the language of symbol and metaphor: being born from above or being born again, living water, bread of life, and so on—no wonder people routinely fail to follow along. Among the Gospels, John alone contains no parables. Jesus is famous for his quick one-liners: "Let the dead bury their own dead" (Luke 9:60), or "All who lift themselves up will be brought low, and those who make themselves low will be lifted up" (Luke 14:11). Sometimes Jesus answers questions with questions. Asked what one must do to inherit eternal life, Jesus bounces the question right back: "What is written in the law?

Introduction

How do you interpret it?" (Luke 10:26). On occasion Jesus dodges a tricky question with an evasive nonanswer. Should we pay taxes to the emperor or not? "Give to Caesar what belongs to Caesar and to God what belongs to God" (Mark 12:17).

For generations, Christians have understood Jesus to have given the safe answer, the moderate answer. We can serve God, and we can serve the government—no conflict. But if we know anything about Caesar, we know that's not what Jesus is doing. Because if you ask Caesar, *What belongs to Caesar?* Caesar will tell you, *Everything belongs to Caesar.* (I use saltier language in my seminary classes.) Once you've given Caesar what he demands, what's left over for God?

Oh.

Jesus provides neither the safe answer nor the moderate answer. Nor does he choose the clear answer. In Mark 12 and in the parallel accounts Jesus has perfectly good reasons for making a clear point without communicating clearly: he does not want to commit treason.

The parables constitute the largest and most distinctive body of Jesus' teachings—and perhaps the most commonly misunderstood. Depending on who's doing the counting, Matthew, Mark, and Luke include between thirty and forty parables. These include some of the most beloved material in the entire Bible, including the Prodigal Son, the Good Samaritan, the Sheep and the Goats, the Treasure Hidden in the Field, the Persistent Widow, the Mustard Seed, the Laborers in the Vineyard, the Lost Sheep, and the Rich Man and Lazarus.

Most of the parables amount to short stories—fairly simple, with few characters and memorable plots. But some of the parables are little more than direct points of comparison, with little to no narrative component. Luke is prone to provide us with memorable characters who think out loud. We all remember the dishonest manager who deliberates, "What will I do now that my master is firing me as his manager? I'm not strong enough to dig and too proud to beg" (16:3). This scoundrel might not make the most desirable friend, but there's something compelling about him. Perhaps we're more likely to empathize with the Prodigal's determination, "I will get up and go to my father, and say to him, 'Father, I have sinned against heaven and against you. I no longer deserve to be called your son. Take me on as one of your hired hands'" (15:18-19).

Introduction

Jesus' parables are often misunderstood for several reasons. First, because too many preachers rush to tame Jesus by oversimplifying his message. "Parables are earthly stories with heavenly meanings," they intone, as if we could boil down Jesus' teachings into nifty illustrations about how to win in the afterlife. As we'll see, Jesus was far edgier than that, far more committed to God's work in the world we live in now.

Second, Jesus' parables generally have what I call a "hook," a point at which the story jumps off the rails of normalcy. Jesus' parables start out with ordinary things. A man is traveling down a road. A woman brings a complaint before a judge. A slave is working in a field. Most of the time, however, things jump off track. I call this moment in the parable the hook. Way back in 1935, the English scholar C. H. Dodd defined the parable this way:

> At its simplest, the parable is a metaphor or simile drawn from nature or common life, arresting the hearer by its vividness or strangeness, and leaving the mind in sufficient doubt to its precise application to tease the mind into active thought.[1]

No definition can satisfy everyone, but Dodd's calls attention to how Jesus' parables have a way of moving from the ordinary to the strange.

Let's consider just a couple of examples.

A woman is baking bread (Matthew 13:33; see Luke 13:20-21). So far, so good. Then she *hides* yeast in a *bushel* of flour. Now we pause. "Hiding" is a strange choice of words for mixing in yeast. A bushel of flour is an extraordinary amount. Questions begin to multiply. Why does she hide the yeast? And "a bushel" of flour?—what ordinary kitchen could possibly accommodate bread baked with a bushel of flour? Is she trying to blow up the house? And how is this process of hiding yeast in such an enormous amount of flour "like" the kingdom of heaven? We have jumped the tracks.

Now, some commentators will say we are pressing the details of this parable too far, making interpretive mountains out of molehills. The point is simple, they say. Jesus is making a simple point about growth. The kingdom of heaven is like leaven. It doesn't take much leaven to transform flatbread into yeast rolls. It is a mistake to overemphasize the woman hiding the yeast, an overactive imagination conjuring up an exploding kitchen.

One more example: in the same chapter of Matthew, Jesus compares the kingdom of heaven to a man who finds hidden treasure in a field, sells everything he owns, and then purchases the field (13:44). Of course he's "full of joy," he's just made himself a fortune. According to many interpreters, that's all there is to say: the things of God are worth our whole lives.

Other interpreters, and I'm one, won't let go of some pesky details. Like little dogs that don't realize how small they really are, we just won't let go of the bone. Something smells fishy about a person who buys property on false pretenses. (Smelly fish come two parables later, in 13:47-50.) It's one thing to be the smart guy who finds the treasure and makes the purchase. But imagine you're the landowner who *sells* the property, totally clueless as to its true value. Again, not only did your buyer find the treasure on your property—how'd *that* happen?—the sorry dog also *hid* it. (There's the motif of hiding it again.) Is the buyer not morally responsible for covering up the found treasure?

Again, interpreters go round and round on this detail. I do not pretend to know what Jesus or the author of Matthew's Gospel had in mind. But I do know this: I know how the seller of the property would likely feel about the purchaser. And that image lies at the heart of this parable. "The kingdom of heaven is like that," Jesus says.

I suggest that many of Jesus' parables have a hook, something strange or off-key that gives us readers lots to talk about. This strange dimension of Jesus' parables may distinguish them from other parables in the ancient world.

Ancient Jews knew what parables were. They knew them from Israel's Scriptures, perhaps most famously when the prophet Nathan confronts King David. Peering from his rooftop, David spotted Bathsheba bathing in her courtyard, sent guards to bring her into his household, and used her sexually. Her ensuing pregnancy implicated the king in a scandal, so David set up Bathsheba's husband, Uriah, to die in battle—a murder, only by the hands of other men. (Nowhere does the Bible depict this as a love affair. Bathsheba shows neither attraction nor devotion to David.)

God sends the prophet Nathan to the king, and Nathan spins a story—a parable, it turns out—about a rich man who took a beloved lamb from his poor neighbor in order to butcher it and use it as dinner for his guest. When David condemns the rich man and imposes a fine, Nathan exclaims: "You are that man!" (2 Samuel 12:7).

David understands the lesson—"I've sinned against the LORD!" (12:13). And that's how Hebrew and Jewish parables generally go. Even after the time of Jesus, the rabbis also told parables with similarly pointed lessons.

Ancient Greek and Roman orators also practice parables, or comparisons. There's something inherently creative in the practice of building a comparison: it causes both author and reader/hearer to build a connection between things that are unlike one another. But there's something different about Jesus' parables too. Let's consider a parable from Book 11 of the *Iliad*.

> As when a river in flood
> From mountain snowfields reaches the flat land
> Whipped by a storm of rain, it sweeps away
> Hundreds of withered oaks, hundreds of pines,
> And casts black tons of driftwood into the sea,
> So Aías in his glory swept the field.[2]

Excellent writing, certainly, but the point is sure: the charging Aías is like a flood, destroying everything in his path. There's not much else to say—or to imagine.

We cannot pin down an exact parallel to Jesus' parables. We historians are ever-suspicious of claims to uniqueness, but the Gospel parables have no exact match in ancient literature.

Recently, however, some scholars have begun to question whether Jesus spoke in parables at all. We have already noted that John's Gospel includes no parables, an odd omission if parables were so distinctive to Jesus' ministry. We've also seen that each Gospel has its own way of presenting Jesus' parables. Luke tends to develop complicated characters with internal motivations. Luke also tends to interpret the parables for us by placing them in certain settings or by telling us what they mean. Mark uses some parables as weapons: aiming them against Jesus' opponents. And Matthew seems particularly fond of parables with final judgment imagery. For these reasons some interpreters doubt that we will ever get beneath the parables to the authentic voice of Jesus.

Introduction

We should not expect the Gospels to report what Jesus said word for word, but neither should we abandon the possibility of hearing Jesus' voice through the parables. The Gospels capture the impression Jesus left upon the movement that worshipped and followed him. They reflect the ways in which early Christians remembered Jesus, the kinds of stories they passed along about him, and the ways those stories clustered together over time. One of the things that comes through most consistently about Jesus is that his teaching often left people at a loss for words. Jesus could be very direct—don't practice religion in order to draw attention (Matthew 6:1)—but the Gospels also reflect how much people struggled to understand him. Even the disciples find themselves asking Jesus about the parables (Mark 4:10; Matthew 13:10; Luke 8:9).

It should not surprise us that each Gospel portrays Jesus in its own way. Indeed, early Christians treasured the diversity among the four Gospels. A second-century believer named Tatian attempted to reduce the four Gospels to a single story—no contradictions! But the church largely rejected that version of the Gospel on the grounds that the Gospels' diversity enriched the church's testimony to Jesus. We might imagine this diversity like appreciating music with a good stereo: there's just so much more to appreciate once we notice it. This diversity authorizes us to interpret the parables together with a measure of curiosity and freedom, perhaps as parables are meant to be experienced.

Chapter 1

Divine Inefficiencies

The Parable of the Soils

Jesus began to teach beside the lake again. Such a large crowd gathered that he climbed into a boat there on the lake. He sat in the boat while the whole crowd was nearby on the shore. He said many things to them in parables. While teaching them, he said, "Listen to this! A farmer went out to scatter seed. As he was scattering seed, some fell on the path; and the birds came and ate it. Other seed fell on rocky ground where the soil was shallow. They sprouted immediately because the soil wasn't deep. When the sun came up, it scorched the plants; and they dried up because they had no roots. Other seed fell among thorny plants. The thorny plants grew and choked the seeds, and they produced nothing. Other seed fell into good soil and bore fruit. Upon growing and increasing, the seed produced in one case a yield of thirty to one, in another case a yield of sixty to one, and in another case a yield of one hundred to one." He said, "Whoever has ears to listen should pay attention!"

Mark 4:1-9

The Parable of the Soils (Mark 4:1-20) offers a promising starting point for several reasons. First, most scholars believe Mark is the earliest of the Gospels, and Mark 4:1-9 is the first parable to appear in

1

Mark. Second, Mark 4:13-20 presents an interpretation of the parable itself—how convenient! Third, in Mark 4:10-12 the disciples ask Jesus why he teaches in parables, and he provides an answer.

In short, we have the first major parable to appear in the earliest Gospel, a fully developed interpretation of that parable, and an account for why Jesus teaches in parables. Imagining this study of Jesus' parables as a medium-range hike, surely we are getting off on the right foot.

In important ways, that is precisely the case: for all these reasons the Parable of the Sower is well-suited to launch our conversations, but it comes with hidden benefits. The parable also opens vexing questions of its own. Jesus' explanation concerning the purpose of his parables not only continues to spur debates among commentators, it also provokes the authors of Matthew and Luke. Even the interpretation Jesus provides for this parable gives us lots to talk about.

Allegories

The Parable of the Sower, labeled the Parable of the Soils in the Common English Bible, is an allegory. Key elements of an allegory correspond to other realities beyond the world of the story. The United States flag provides an example: thirteen stripes for each of the original colonies, fifty stars for each of the fifty states. In the Parable of the Sower, the seed corresponds to the "word," while each kind of soil indicates different responses to the word.

My college required almost every student to take the same two-year interdisciplinary humanities class. A common rite of passage for first-year students involved an encounter with the "Allegory of the Cave" from Plato's *Republic*. Plato imagines people who are trapped in a cave. They can see only figures on a wall, shadows of objects that pass between a fire that is lit behind them and themselves. They have no other access to reality. Imagine, Plato challenges us, that one of these people should escape their chains, pass out of the cave into broad daylight, and try to report reality as it is beyond the cave to their fellow lifelong cave dwellers. Should that person try to drag their companions out of the cave, their former companions might even kill them.

Plato's example reveals that the basic terms of an allegory may be fairly simple: one set of terms corresponds to another set of ideas in straightforward ways. But as generations of philosophers and college students will attest, the significance of those allegories often proves far more subtle.

Many of us grew up hearing that Jesus used parables as simple teaching lessons. What if he didn't? Having read the Gospels and mounds of research on the historical Jesus, the journalist Adam Gopnik describes Jesus as "verbally spry and even a little shifty," prone to "defiant, enigmatic paradoxes and pregnant parables that never quite close, perhaps by design."[1]

Gopnik characterizes a Jesus who engages in high-stakes verbal combat with his opponents, often using parables and snappy one-liners as weapons in such hostile exchanges. Seminary students frequently notice how rarely anyone understands Jesus in the Gospel stories. Remarkably, the people most likely to understand Jesus are the ones who, speaking theoretically, should struggle to do so. Sinners and tax collectors follow along just fine (Luke 15:1-2), and the people he heals generally understand without much problem. The struggling comes from would-be disciples and from the supposedly righteous. But Jesus rarely comes off as easy to understand.

I have dedicated this study to Charles Melchert, one of my best friends. Melchert, a biblical scholar and Christian educator, raises the question, "Why didn't Jesus tell Bible stories?" In other words, why do so many of Jesus' teachings require his disciples to use their own imaginations, draw their own inferences, and make their own judgments? Why does Jesus so rarely tie the bow of learning for his followers like we expect modern teachers to do?[2]

Perhaps our problem lies in what we expect from teaching—and from learning. We often think of teaching in terms of what we teach. Regarding the teaching activity of Jesus, Melchert poses different questions: What is worth learning? How is learning evoked? What is the point of learning in a certain way?

The Parable of the Soils may be an allegory. Most of Jesus' parables are not. And if we keep in mind that Jesus rarely taught in order to deliver straightforward Sunday School lessons, we may find that this parable, too, especially tied to its interpretation, will pose its own challenges for us.

Structure

Mark 4:1-20 presents a fairly straightforward structure. We have a setting: A crowd gathers around Jesus, so he teaches them from a boat while they remain ashore (4:1-2). Then Jesus shares the parable, concluding with an exhortation to understand (4:3-9). During some alone time with his followers, including the twelve, Jesus explains why he teaches in parables (4:10-12), then explains this particular parable (4:13-20).

The parable itself and the interpretation that follows it have four major sections each, and each section is defined by a kind of soil. The final type of soil, called "the good soil," receives a little more attention than do the other kinds. We might represent the passage like this.

> Setting: Jesus delivers parables from a boat (4:1-2)
> Parable (4:3-9)
> > Listen! A farmer scatters (4:3)
> > Soil #1: the path (4:4)
> > Soil #2: rocky ground (4:5-6)
> > Soil #3: among thorns (4:7)
> > Soil #4: good soil (4:8)
> > Pay attention! (4:9)
> Interchange about the parables (4:10-12)
> Interpretation (4:13-20)
> "Don't you understand this parable?" (4:13) The farmer scatters *the word* (4:14)
> > Soil #1: the path (4:15)
> > Soil #2: rocky ground (4:16-17)
> > Soil #3: among thorns (4:17-18)
> > Soil #4: good soil (4:19-20)

The structure of Mark 4:1-20 is simple enough, as the interpretation mirrors the parable, but the larger context raises one problem. Jesus begins the parable by addressing a big crowd (4:1-2). Then he speaks to a smaller circle of his own followers (4:10-20). Jesus goes on with even more parables after explaining this parable to his disciples (4:21-32), and it appears that he is again addressing the large crowd. Mark concludes the section by telling us that Jesus "explained everything to his disciples when he was alone with them" (4:34)—but Mark has never alerted us to these changes in audience!

Sowers

They say familiarity breeds contempt. In my experience that saying applies with double force to Jesus' parables, for we think we know what to expect when that may not be the case at all. When it comes to the Parable of the Soils, we rarely pause to investigate one detail: the sower/farmer casts seed on a path, on shallow soil, and among thorns. What reasonable farmer would cast most of his seed on unpromising soil?

To a modern reader, it seems our farmer is a model of inefficiency. Sure enough, interpreters grasp precisely upon this point.

Some interpreters regard the sower's apparent carelessness as crucial to the parable, its "hook." Agrarian audiences have no patience with farmers who squander scarce resources like seed. Careless farmless don't survive for long. A sower who scatters seed in unpromising soil opens us to wonder. Does God scatter the good news even in the most unpromising places, regardless of the likely outcomes? Perhaps God is more generous than we might imagine, willing to "waste" the divine resources even among the most unlikely of us. That would be good news indeed.

A second class of interpreters would say that we're making mountains out of molehills. The parable isn't *about* farming, they would say. Instead, the parable *uses* farming to help us think *about* responses to the word. We should leave behind the sowing metaphor and begin to think about responses to the word and the amazing growth that occurs among the good soil. That's where the true wonder lies.

A third option presents itself. Modern farmers have soil down to a science. They can send their soil samples to the labs at Penn State, Auburn, or Texas A&M, and they know what kinds of seed will grow in what kinds of soil. But ancient farmers lacked that kind of technology, as farmers in some less technologically advanced societies do today. They might not know whether soil was good or bad until their crops came in.

We can appreciate this parable without specialized information about ancient farming practices. Sometimes cultural information from the biblical world will greatly enhance our appreciation of the parables. With the Sower and the Soil, however, the audience does not have to wait until the harvest to see how things turn out. Jesus tells us right from the top what to expect: the sower sows on the path, on rocky soil, and among thorny plants. More precisely, Jesus says, the seed "falls" in these places: the visual image is that the sower is just tossing seed around.

How fortunate that some of the seed "fell into good soil and bore fruit" (4:8). As readers we are left to ponder twin mysteries: a Sower who scatters seed that has little chance of bearing good fruit, along with the wonder of a bountiful yield.

Secrets, Mysteries, and the Nature of the Kingdom

What if Mark had shared Jesus' parable alone with no reaction from the disciples and no explanation from Jesus? Chances are, the Parable of the Sower and the Soil would not stand among those we remember particularly well.

We remember this parable especially because of the interchange between Jesus and the disciples. Mark's version of that conversation stands out in particular, but we should consider it alongside those of Matthew and Luke.

Matthew 13:10-17	Mark 4:10-12	Luke 8:9-10
Jesus' disciples came and said to him, "Why do you use parables when you speak to the crowds?" Jesus replied, "Because they haven't received the secrets of the kingdom of heaven, but you have. For those who have will receive more and they will have more than enough. But as for those who don't have, even the little they have will be taken away from them. This is why I speak to the crowds in parables: although they see, they don't really	When they were alone, the people around Jesus, along with the Twelve, asked him about the parables. He said to them, "The secret of God's kingdom has been given to you, but to those who are outside everything comes in parables. This is so that they can look and see but have no insight, and they can hear but not understand. Otherwise, they might turn their lives around and be forgiven.	His disciples asked him what this parable meant. He said, "You have been given the mysteries of God's kingdom, but these mysteries come to everyone else in parables so that when they see, they can't see, and when they hear, they can't understand."

6

see; and although they hear, they don't really hear or understand. What Isaiah prophesied has become completely true for them: You will hear, to be sure, but never understand; and you will certainly see but never recognize what you are seeing. For this people's senses have become calloused, and they've become hard of hearing, and they've shut their eyes so that they won't see with their eyes or hear with their ears or understand with their minds, and change their hearts and lives that I may heal them. *"Happy are your eyes because they see. Happy are your ears because they hear. I assure you that many prophets and righteous people wanted to see what you see and hear what you hear, but they didn't."*		

A lot is going on here. Most obviously, Matthew presents us with many more words than Mark does, while Luke offers fewer.

But let's start with Mark. The disciples ask Jesus why he speaks in parables, and Jesus replies that he uses parables so that those outside will fail to understand. The parables, then, discriminate between insiders and outsiders. Insiders should understand what Jesus means, but outsiders will find the parables frustrating or confusing.

This passage may pose a problem for many of us. For one thing, we've often heard that Jesus used parables to help people understand his message. We're used to thinking of parables like nifty teaching illustrations that make a point simple—if not simple, then at least easy to understand. We know George Washington was honest because he confessed to having cut down the cherry tree as a child. Maybe Parson Weems made up the story, but it conveyed a simple point and it was memorable. "I cannot tell a lie," said little George. Surely parables work like that. But, Mark says, parables do not work like that. They raise barriers that prevent outsiders from understanding.

Unlike ancient people, modern readers assume that important truths should be shared. Meditation lowers blood pressure, raises happiness levels, and extends life expectancies: we should start a marketing campaign and promote mindfulness in the workplace! Not everyone holds this value, whether around the world or throughout history. Some cultures regard wisdom as appropriate only for the worthy, and so it is with much of the biblical tradition. In Proverbs, Lady Wisdom warns potential instructors not to waste their efforts on unworthy students who will only hurt their teachers; instead teachers should devote themselves to the wise, who will take advantage of their instruction (9:7-9). Jesus himself warns disciples against tossing holy things to dogs and throwing pearls in front of pigs (Matthew 7:6).

The authors of Matthew and Luke apparently had reservations. Most agree that the authors of Matthew and Luke based their Gospels on Mark's. Matthew and Luke include most of Mark's stories, tell the stories with largely the same words, and share the stories in basically the same order. In other words, Mark's account provides the common structure upon which the stories of Matthew and Luke build—Matthew more so than Luke.

However, Matthew and Luke will change Mark's version for various reasons, some stylistic and some thematic or even theological. In this case, Luke basically follows Mark's wording but shortens Mark. This is a trend: If we follow Mark story by story, it seems Matthew and Luke find Mark too wordy: they tend to shorten Mark's accounts. Luke shortens Mark's version but keeps Mark's basic logic: the parables allow outsiders to hear Jesus' words without understanding their full meaning. Luke makes one omission, however, that may be more significant than it looks. Mark is drawing from Isaiah: "Otherwise, they might turn their lives around and be forgiven" (see Isaiah 6:9-10). Luke omits this line, perhaps leaving open the possibility that even outsiders might find forgiveness. Indeed, the larger story of Luke's Gospel seems a little more open to that possibility than Mark does.

But Matthew seems a lot more concerned about Mark's account. Matthew's main change involves substituting one three-letter Greek word for another. In English, where Mark says Jesus uses parables "so that" outsiders will not comprehend, Matthew says "that is why" Jesus resorts to parables. Matthew shifts the responsibility for the misunderstanding from Jesus to the outsiders. Then Matthew does what Matthew typically does. Where Mark may mention or even quote from the Hebrew Scriptures, Matthew provides a full citation: Isaiah predicted this is what would happen. About a dozen such citations occur in Matthew. In their own ways, Matthew and Luke both show some discomfort with the explanation Jesus provides for the parables in Mark.

But a funny thing happens. Although they are now insiders who have received the secret of God's kingdom, the disciples still don't understand this parable. They need Jesus to explain it to them. They're not such great insiders after all.

All four Gospels characterize the disciples as a mixed success. They leave everything to follow Jesus. Sometimes they follow his instructions. Sometimes their fear overwhelms them. Sometimes they act impulsively. Often they will fail to understand Jesus. For his part, Jesus will never fail the disciples whether they succeed or fail. In Mark the disciples will go out on mission; they will even perform healings and exorcisms. But Mark goes especially tough on the disciples. In the end the disciples all abandon Jesus, running away frightened—and Mark describes no moment at which the risen Jesus appears to them. Mark simply concludes with the promise that Jesus will appear to them and they will bear the gospel (13:9-13; 14:28; 16:7). All of that lies beyond the boundaries of Mark's story. At the end of the Gospel they have failed, and only the promise abides.

Explaining a Parable

It's terrible when we have to explain our jokes. I know the pain more than most. My humor is always half a step off, so I often have to retrace my steps. Pride wounded, I console myself with the thought that my friends just sometimes can't keep up with my fast-paced wit. Yeah, that's it.

Unfortunately, I have children who interpret things differently.

Jesus seems to find it frustrating that he must explain the Parable of the Soils to his disciples: "Don't you understand the parable?" Mark's Gospel sometimes explains Jesus' emotions to us. He can be angry (1:41; 10:14), appalled (6:6), compassionate (6:34; 8:2), frustrated (7:24), impatient (8:12), loving (10:21), and distressed (14:33). In this way Mark stands out among biblical storytellers, who rarely give away the emotions of the characters in their stories—yet Mark does so less than many modern writers would. In Mark 4:13 we are reading between the lines when we attribute frustration to Jesus. He has just congratulated the disciples for receiving the secret, yet he must explain his parable to them.

Jesus does not need to explain all his parables. He shares several more in Mark 4. Several seem to underscore the message of the Sower and the Soil. Jesus shares a parable about seed that grows "all by itself" (4:26-29), echoing the abundant growth produced by the good soil. The Parable of the Mustard Seed raises questions that vex professional interpreters, but the motif of spectacular growth carries through there as well (4:30-32). Wonder at the process of natural growth and abundance is a prominent theme in Mark 4.

The Mustard Seed: Simple or Complicated?

Through the centuries, interpreters have generally received the Parable of the Mustard Seed (4:30-32) as a straightforward illustration of the Kingdom's bountiful growth. Jesus compares the kingdom of God to a mustard seed, "the smallest of all the seeds on the earth," that grows into an impressive plant, even providing shelter for birds. Mustard may not be the world's smallest seed, but it is small enough, and it does grow into an impressive plant. Naturally, ancient Christians applied Jesus' image to the growth of the church.

Some recent interpreters perceive more subversive elements in Jesus' parable. Mustard can be regarded as a weed, after all, and no farmer wants birds coming to nest in their fields. Jesus *could* have compared the kingdom of God to a giant cedar tree, which evokes wonder in everyone who sees it—but instead he chose a troublesome plant that produces a pungent condiment. Perhaps, these interpreters argue, Jesus is suggesting that the kingdom of God has a way of insinuating itself in inconvenient ways.

Divine Inefficiencies

One other parable in the chapter also involves growth and abundance, but it brings a different edge. Jesus says, "God will evaluate you with the same standard you use to evaluate others" (4:24). That doesn't sound much like a parable, but a more literal rendering would be: "By the measure with which you measure, shall it be measured to you." ("God" and "others" are absent from Jesus' sentence in Greek.) This sounds much more like a parable, inviting listeners to compare their own standards of assessment with the ways of God. And, Jesus adds,

> You will receive even more. Those who have will receive more, but as for those who don't have, even what they don't have will be taken away from them.
>
> Mark 4:24c-25

These concluding words resonate with the motif of the soil. Some kinds of soil simply lack the capacity to generate a harvest, while others produce abundantly.

Jesus' explanation begins by explaining the seed. The Common English Bible renders Jesus' opening statement this way: "The farmer scatters the word" (4:14). More literally, the Greek text reads: "The sower sows the word," which is how most other translations read. Every translation works according to its own translation theory. The CEB seeks to avoid confusing its readers, and in this instance the translators are basically correct. In Mark's Gospel, Jesus' basic message concerns his announcement that the kingdom of God is breaking into the world. Jesus brings this message right at the beginning of this ministry: "Now is the time! Here comes God's kingdom! Change your hearts and lives, and trust this good news!" (1:14-15). Other parables in Mark 4 discuss the kingdom of God.

The kingdom of God must look very much like Jesus' ministry. Mark provides no other context for understanding it. While human "kings" rule by domination and exploitation, God's rule brings healing, community, and justice. We see Jesus performing healings, casting out evil spirits, gathering communities of disciples, and building networks of followers throughout Galilee and then Judea—all of them living in this way of love. The word of the kingdom must look like the word Jesus lives out.

Why Do Bible Translations Differ?

People often express concern about differences among Bible translations. Pick up two translations of any book, and you'll notice how different they are, usually more different than your translations of the Bible. The committees of scholars who translate the Bible begin with philosophies about how language works. For example, does meaning happen at the level of individual words or in clauses and sentences? What do we do with words that have different meanings in different contexts? Do we use gender-inclusive language when authors seem to have intended to address women as well as men but only used masculine pronouns like "he" or "him"?

Translation committees also worry about their readers. They must choose an English reading level, which determines sentence structure and vocabulary. Will they explain complicated terms (like "word" in Mark 4:14), or leave the work to the reader? Will they use English profanity for Hebrew or Greek profanity? In the end, all the major modern English translations are basically reliable. They differ from one another for reasons that are easy to understand.

This parable raises a potential crisis for Jesus' listeners—and for us. The parable, alongside Jesus' explanation of it, sets forth four kinds of soil, and three are unproductive. Especially with the interpretation Jesus provides in 4:13-20, the three unproductive soils may provide a key for understanding Mark's characters.[3] They also present a challenging mirror for those of us who take Mark's story to heart.

Mark's story is full of characters who show no positive response to Jesus, those who correspond to the path or road. We should imagine not a road paved with stones but a well-worn path, where the soil is packed down hard. The seed has no chance to settle in, nowhere to sprout or take root. The seed simply remains on the surface, ready to be plucked up by anyone. In Mark that role is readily supplied by Jesus' opponents, who confront him from the beginning and never relent.

Scribes, Pharisees, Sadducees: What Do We Know?

The Gospels confront Jesus with a variety of opponents: scribes, Pharisees, Sadducees, Herodians, and priests. Each Gospel characterizes these groups in its own way. For example, Jesus has some friendly interactions with Pharisees in Luke and John but not in Matthew or Mark. We have some knowledge of these groups from sources beyond the Gospels. The apostle Paul describes himself as a Pharisee. However, we know far less about their lives, their social contexts, their beliefs, and their activities than we would like.

The Gospels themselves are a problem. By the time the Gospels were written, all or most of these groups no longer existed. The Jewish Revolt against Rome had ended in disaster, and the social structure of Roman Palestine was forever changed. Those who first heard the Gospels read aloud may never have met a real Sadducee or had any interest in what one was like. This means modern readers must keep in mind that the scribes, Pharisees, and Sadducees we encounter in the Gospels may or may not resemble the people with whom Jesus interacted. Like movie villains, they have roles to play in the story.

As early as chapter 2, Jesus encounters "legal experts," or scribes. Mark has already contrasted Jesus' teaching with that of the scribes (1:22), for Jesus speaks on his own authority. We don't know as much as we might like to about scribes during the time of Jesus. Presumably they served some sort of public or clerical purpose, their authority resting upon institutional privilege rather than personal insight or charisma. Remarkably, in their first meeting, Jesus is the one to initiate conflict with them. People lower their paralyzed friend through the roof of a house, and instead of simply healing the man, Jesus begins by doing what only God should do, forgiving the man's sins. No wonder the scribes are offended! The scribes and the Pharisees unite against Jesus in early conflicts, along with a group called the Herodians. Very early in Mark, the Herodians and the Pharisees already seek to have Jesus killed (3:6).

Jesus makes even more enemies when he arrives in Jerusalem. There he encounters the people who administer the Temple, Israel's holiest place. There priests offered sacrifices to God and exerted a measure of Jewish self-rule under Roman supervision. The chief priests, elders, and Sadducees enter Mark's story only here, and it is they who see to Jesus' arrest. Mark shows us no positive interactions between Jesus and these groups. Like the seed falling on the path, nothing good sprouts from these interactions.

The second kind of soil is more complicated—and therefore more relevant for us today. Rocky soil might have a nice layer of dirt on top, but it's too thin. The root can't settle in, so the plant cannot thrive. Under pressure like persecution, this second kind of plant will fall away because it lacks the root structure to endure.

Mark's Gospel features a prominent character with a "rocky" name: Simon Peter. The Greek name *Petros* refers to a small stone or pebble. Perhaps it is unfair to say of Peter that he has "no roots" or that he lasts "only a little while" (4:17). He responds immediately when Jesus calls him (1:16-18), and he follows Jesus wherever he goes. Peter, like the others, has left everything to follow Jesus (10:28). Chosen among the twelve apostles, Peter also figures with James and John in Jesus' closest circle of male followers. He alone recognizes Jesus as the Messiah, although he fails to comprehend what that entails for Jesus (8:29-33), and he is present for the transfiguration, again failing to grasp exactly what to make of things (9:2-8). Peter fails to stay alert during Jesus' time of trial (14:37); worse, he denies knowing Jesus after Jesus' arrest (14:66-72). Like the other disciples, Peter abandons Jesus when his teacher is arrested, yet Jesus does not give up on Peter. Peter will receive word of the Resurrection (16:7).

Like the seed that falls on rocky soil, Peter fails Jesus when things get hard. He does well at first, spectacularly so on some occasions. In the end, however, Peter runs away scared and will not declare his allegiance. But Jesus does not fail Peter.

Mark does not leave the question of rocky soil with Peter. For Mark, discipleship means risk. Jesus warns potential disciples explicitly: whoever wants to follow Jesus must take up a cross of their own (8:34). Disciples will face betrayal, abandonment, and trial. Salvation requires staying faithful all the way to the end (13:9-13). Would-be disciples might see our own reflection in Peter: will an early determination to follow Jesus, and even some initial success, see its way through to the end?

The third soil poses more complicated challenges. At first glance, it seems only a few characters in Mark resemble the seed falling among thornbushes, those who hear the word but are more concerned with wealth and other worldly affairs (4:18-19). The first character who comes to mind would be the rich man who asks Jesus what he must do to receive eternal life (10:17-22). When Jesus reminds the man of the commandments, there's no problem: the man has kept these his whole adult life.

One wonders: was Jesus not sincere in his first reply? Looking at the man again and loving him, Jesus appraises him differently. This man must sell everything he owns, give the proceeds to the poor, then follow Jesus. This is too much for the man because he is very rich.

Few of us would describe ourselves as "very rich," but many of us fear that our lifestyles might not conform to Jesus' call. A closer look at Mark might increase our discomfort, for there are other characters who perhaps begin well but worry too much what others think—and they are surprising. What about Herod, who holds mixed opinions about John the Baptist? On the one hand, he keeps John imprisoned because he cannot tolerate John's condemnation of his incestuous/adulterous marriage. On the other hand, he treats John as a sort of mascot: not only is he afraid to harm John due to the preacher's personal righteousness, he actually *enjoys* John's preaching. Herod orders John's execution only because he has made a rash public promise: Herod must save face, and he regrets it (6:14-29). Concern for status outweighs concern for justice, and that's just too bad for John.

And what of Pontius Pilate, the Roman governor who finds Jesus innocent yet sends him to his death? Pilate discerns that the chief priests have referred Jesus' case to him out of false motives (15:10). His efforts to rally the crowd to Jesus' defense have failed, even when he calls Jesus the so-called "king of the Jews" (15:12-14). So now Pilate chooses to please the crowd (15:15). What Mark doesn't say— and what ancient readers didn't need to be told—is that Pilate's job depended upon his keeping the peace, so Pilate sends Jesus off to the cross against his own better judgment. He starts "worrying about the needs of this life," as Jesus says (4:19).

Contemporary readers readily identify with the rich man, a person who is basically decent but who stumbles before the radical demand to divest himself of his positions and pursue Jesus' itinerant lifestyle. Most of us find it harder to imagine our affinity with Herod or Pilate, cruel tyrants both, and understandably so. Our aversion to Pilate and to Herod masks the kind of truth we prefer to avoid: we'll do most anything to keep things under control, to manage others' perceptions, to hang on to our status, to save face in the face of possible embarrassment. How deeply are we corrupted by our desires to keep all those affairs within some semblance of order?

One of the more effective, yet underreported, strategies of the civil rights movement involved "kneel-ins." Groups of African American Christians, often mixed with white colleagues, would appear at white churches unannounced in hopes of worshipping with white congregations. Sometimes these delegations would receive welcome. Sometimes they would be allowed to worship in restricted areas. And sometimes they would be excluded.

Historian Stephen R. Haynes has documented how important it became for segregationist churches to save face while excluding these fellow Christians from worship. Haynes chronicles how an elder of one Birmingham church responded to a pastor who appealed to Christian principles in 1963: "To hell with Christian principles—we've got to save the church!" In 1964 an elder in Tuskegee replied to his pastor, "Leave the Bible out of this. Read *The Rise and Fall of the Roman Empire*, and you'll see what's happening here."[4] We "good Christians" can find ourselves saying and doing repulsive things in order to protect things that matter to us.

There are more kinds of bad soil than good, more ways not to become fruitful than to result in a harvest. One aspect of the Parable of the Soils challenges listeners to examine the three kinds of unproductive soil and perhaps to examine themselves. What obstacles prevent us from yielding a bountiful harvest? Perhaps a careful accounting of this question will produce surprising results.

Bounty

The miracle of agriculture is that little seeds produce great crops. They take in water, sunlight, and nutrients, and they grow way beyond the tininess of their original state. I'm not much of a gardener myself, but I imagine this is one of the factors that leads friends to take up gardening as a hobby.

When Jesus describes a thirty-, sixty-, or even a hundred-fold harvest, he's saying nothing shocking or surprising to his agrarian audience. Little seeds make great harvests. But if we're talking about the word, the message of God's work in the world, are our imaginations ready for a great yield? Thirty-, sixty-, or a hundred-fold, Jesus suggests. Spreading the word will have its way in good soil, whether we are ready or not.

One handy rule of interpretation reminds us that things could always be different. Throughout this study, we will avoid literal thinking while taking the parables seriously in their details. Jesus suggests three different bountiful yields, increasing in their richness. I would suggest Jesus is encouraging his readers to open their imaginations: maybe thirty, maybe sixty, maybe a hundred, who knows? Such an intent would be consistent with other parables in Mark 4 that evoke wonder at growth that simply happens apart from human effort. God's work in the world is bountiful.

Always Misunderstood?

We have seen that Jesus congratulates his disciples as recipients of the kingdom's secret, using parables so that outsiders will remain confused. Yet the disciples still don't understand the Parable of the Soils, and Jesus provides them with an explanation.

It is not always the case that Jesus' parables elude outsiders. Mark's other major parable, the Parable of the Tenant Farmers (12:1-11), resembles the Soils in important ways. A man cultivates a vineyard and leases it to tenants. But when the owner sends enslaved workers to collect his share of the produce, the tenants abuse the messengers. Finally, the owner sends his "one son whom he loved dearly"—but the tenants murder him. In retaliation the owner destroys the tenants and gives the vineyard over to others. Both parables are allegories. The Parable of the Tenant Farmers uses a vineyard as a symbol for Israel and tenants as stand-ins for the authorities who govern within Israel. The "slaves" in the parable represent the prophets sent by God to correct Israel, and the son, whom the tenants kill, obviously has to do with Jesus. Jesus has already predicted his death at the hands of the Temple authorities on three occasions. In Mark's telling "they" understand the point immediately: the parable is directed against "them," and they seek to arrest Jesus.

Within Mark 4, Jesus continues speaking in parables. He has said, "to those who are outside everything comes in parables" (v. 11). So he goes on speaking in parables to the crowds "as much as they were able to hear," explaining everything to his disciples (vv. 33-34). Will they ever reach the point at which they need no further explanation?

Chapter 2

Funny Business

The Parable of the Workers in the Vineyard

"The kingdom of heaven is like a landowner who went out early in the morning to hire workers for his vineyard. After he agreed with the workers to pay them a denarion, he sent them into his vineyard.

"Then he went out around nine in the morning and saw others standing around the marketplace doing nothing. He said to them, 'You also go into the vineyard, and I'll pay you whatever is right.' And they went.

"Again around noon and then at three in the afternoon, he did the same thing. Around five in the afternoon he went and found others standing around, and he said to them, 'Why are you just standing around here doing nothing all day long?'

" 'Because nobody has hired us,' they replied.

"He responded, 'You also go into the vineyard.'

"When evening came, the owner of the vineyard said to his manager, 'Call the workers and give them their wages, beginning with the last ones hired and moving on finally to the first.' When those who were hired at five in the afternoon came, each one received a denarion. Now when those hired first came, they thought they would receive more. But each of them also received a denarion. When they received it, they grumbled against the landowner, 'These who were hired last worked one hour, and they received the same pay as we did even though we had to work the whole day in the hot sun.'

"But he replied to one of them, 'Friend, I did you no wrong. Didn't I agree to pay you a denarion? Take what belongs to you and go. I want to give to this one who was hired last the same as I give to you. Don't I have the right to do what I want with what belongs to me? Or are you resentful because I'm generous?' So those who are last will be first. And those who are first will be last."

Matthew 20:1-16

Assume nothing. If I have learned anything from twenty-five years of teaching in classrooms, and a lot longer teaching in churches, you should learn this: assume nothing about the people in your classroom or study group. You may find some home-cooked Bible experts who know parts of the Bible you've long forgotten, and you may meet people who need the table of contents to find the Gospel of John. Thank God for both groups. But it's best to assume nothing about a group of students: their religious backgrounds, their personal histories, their belief systems.

Matthew's Parable of the Workers in the Vineyard challenges this rule. Some readers will come to the parable with fresh eyes. For those who already know the story, however, there's a very good chance I can predict the interpretations they bring to the conversation.

We'll call the largest group the "Grace" camp. This group regards the parable as a story about grace and salvation, particularly salvation in the sense of getting into heaven.

The second group is smaller. We'll call them the "Justice" camp. For them, the parable is about everyone getting their fair share.

We'll discuss a third thread of interpretation that really doesn't boil down to a "group." It's more a line of thinking that gloms on to other interpretations and involves the relationship between the gospel and its Jewish origins.

Each of these interpretations emphasizes key details of the parable. But each also minimizes—ignores, actually—other key parts. We'll begin by considering this parable in its cultural context, then we'll explore each of these popular interpretations: what aspects of the parable do they call attention do, and what aspects do they neglect?

You know where this is headed. Perhaps the most popular inter-pretations leave out a fairly significant aspect of the story.

Cultural Context

The parable begins with a comparison. By associating the vineyard with the kingdom of heaven, Jesus reminds his hearers of a biblical im-age. On several occasions Isaiah compares Israel to a vineyard, which God has planted and cultivated. Its leaders have exploited it for their own purposes (3:13-15; see Jeremiah 12:10), and it has yielded poor fruit rather than grapes (5:1-7; 27:1-6). The Parable of the Tenant Farmers relies upon this comparison even more directly (Mark 12:1-12; Matthew 21:33-36; Luke 20:9-19). Here the comparison is less expansive: a landowner needs workers for the vineyard and goes to hire them.

The vineyard owner needs workers, so he goes to the marketplace to hire them. He contracts with the workers for a fair wage, suggest-ing that they could decline his offer. Indeed, some of the workers do complain when they receive their pay at the end of the day. Both factors suggest the workers can look the landowner in the eye and speak for themselves. Clearly the landowner needs workers to collect his harvest.

But make no mistake: this is not a relationship among equals. Only one character in the story owns land. Only one has a harvest to collect. After the landowner hires the first bunch of workers early in the morning, still others wait around in the marketplace. This is a factor that often divides modern readers. When the landowner re-turns later in the morning, he finds workers "doing nothing" (20:3). Even late in the afternoon he asks those who remain, "Why are you just standing around here doing nothing all day long?" (20:6). Many readers conclude that these people must be lazy.

But consider their answer. "Because nobody has hired us" (20:7). The situation is that one man needs workers, but the workers appar-ently need work so desperately that they wait all day in the market-place, even after reasonable hope has long passed.

Christian readers have tended to associate the landowner in the Parable of the Workers with God—and for good reason. We have al-ready seen that Jesus introduces the parable in terms of the kingdom of heaven, while the vineyard imagery reminds us of God's relationship with Israel. Also, rabbis told parables centuries after the time of Jesus. We cannot know for certain whether these rabbinic parables go back to parables from Jesus' day, but it's quite common for them to compare God to a king—and a few of them liken God to a king who hires workers. So it comes as no surprise that Christians have routinely read the landowner as God.

The parable itself does not mention a harvest, yet harvest time does seem to be implied. Those workers who labor all day complain about the hot sun (20:12). This may refer to the season for harvesting grapes, which is notoriously hot in Galilee. We should also consider the landowner's strange (to us) hiring practices. Ordinarily, business owners hire enough people to get the job done and let them go when the work is finished, paying them for the amount of work they have completed. The key point is to get all the work done, especially at harvest time when nothing should be left on the vine. Perhaps, expecting that workers hired early in the morning would expect a full days' wage—just as the workers negotiate here (20:2)—a landowner might parcel out work until all the work gets done. But that's a tricky calculation, especially since this landowner winds up paying everyone the same amount anyway. In any case, the workers know to show up in the marketplace, the landowner knows they will be there, and all the work seems to get done during a very hot period of the year.

Early in the morning the landowner agrees to pay the laborers a denarion, a silver coin considered to be a typical day's wage for a laborer. That assumption opens a more basic set of questions. If a denarion was a typical wage, did subsistence require a denarion a day? If it did, what happens to workers who failed to earn a denarion per day, as most of the workers in this parable expect? And would a denarion support just an individual or a small household? Most commentators seem satisfied to report that a denarion is a typical daily wage without taking such basic questions of survival into account. How did ancient workers manage to get by? The honest answer is, we don't know exactly.

Readers face a decision. We can choose a spiritual route, where the material details of labor and wages matter very little. Or we can take those metaphorical facts more seriously, assuming that we should not divorce a parable from its details.

Deathbed Confessions: The Grace Camp

A notorious country gang ruled the area of North Alabama where I grew up. I won't use their names because I'm sure to get some details wrong and because my family still knows some of the principals involved. But people disappeared, bodies were found in the woods, and convictions did occur. People went to prison.

And jailhouse conversions happened. One of the more notorious criminals emerged from prison an evangelist, only to wind up back in prison. His life fulfilled the most common interpretation of the Parable of the Workers in the Vineyard: it's never too late in life for someone to find grace, thereby gaining a spot in heaven.

This classic interpretation revolves around two essential elements in the parable. All the workers receive equal pay, regardless of how many hours they work. Even those who arrive late in the day receive the same wage. And when some workers grumble at this fact, the landowner responds, "Are you resentful because I'm generous?" The parable thus becomes the epitome of divine grace.

In revivalist preaching, the workers who started early in the morning provide the perfect foils for the good news. Their resentment embodies precisely the attitudes preachers want to undermine. The first attitude makes an easy mark: the moral superiority of those who think they have their religion figured out. It's easy to make fun of them and their "works righteousness." A good preacher can spin one example after another of the person who thought themselves superior, only to have their hypocrisy shown up for all to see. The second attitude is more tender. Many people sincerely believe they have made such a mess of their lives that God's grace can never find them. They genuinely regret that they've reached a stage in life at which they are beyond hope. This parable is the evangelist's best friend: "It doesn't matter what you've done, or how late in life you may be." We can imagine the sentimental church music cuing up.

One key element in this interpretation involves the kingdom of heaven. Only Matthew's Gospel uses this phrase. The others use "kingdom of God." Matthew uses both, with a clear preference for "kingdom of heaven."

Matthew probably prefers "kingdom of heaven" out of reverence for the divine name. Matthew's Gospel reflects a thoroughly Jewish form of Jesus devotion, one that maintains fidelity to the Torah, the law of Israel. Only in Matthew does Jesus say,

> Don't even begin to think that I have come to do away with the Law and the Prophets. I haven't come to do away with them but to fulfill them.
>
> Matthew 5:17

And it looks like he means it. So perhaps Matthew uses "kingdom of heaven" simply to minimize using "God." That explanation has its own problems, as Matthew uses the term "God" quite frequently.

Readers in the "grace camp" may associate the kingdom of heaven with, well, heaven: the blessed place people go after we die. If we begin this parable with the assumption that Jesus is talking about how people go to heaven, then it's natural to see the denarion in terms of a final reward, a heavenly destination. No matter how long one spends serving God in this life, a person enjoys the same afterlife. This is good news for sinners. It's frustrating for self-righteous religious people. And it just might make good theology: God's generosity toward humankind exceeds our imaginations.

Savvy readers will have guessed that, since we're discussing the "grace camp" first, this is not the interpretation I will finally recommend. However, let's consider that it has a good deal to recommend it. For one thing, we've mentioned that Matthew's Gospel shows more interest in a final judgment and an afterlife than the other Gospels do. For example, Matthew provides several parables that involve sifting and dividing imagery—many of these come from Matthew alone. These include:

- the Weeds Among the Wheat and its interpretation (13:24-30, 36-43, only in Matthew);
- the Net (13:47-50, only in Matthew);
- the Wedding Party (22:1-14, with details unique to Matthew);
- the Bridesmaids (25:1-13, only in Matthew);

- the Valuable Coins, or Talents (25:14-30; see Luke 19:12-27); and
- the Sheep and the Goats (25:31-46, only in Matthew).

Matthew is also especially fond of "weeping and grinding their teeth" imagery as a way of talking about exclusion from the blessed future, using it six times against just once in Luke. (It never occurs in Mark or John.) Matthew clearly cares about the final judgment and presumably the afterlife.

When Matthew uses "kingdom of heaven," it often seems to point beyond the present moment. For example, in these verses he links "kingdom of heaven" to a final judgment scene.

> "Not everybody who says to me, 'Lord, Lord,' will get into the kingdom of heaven. Only those who do the will of my Father who is in heaven will enter. On the Judgment Day, many people will say to me, 'Lord, Lord, didn't we prophesy in your name and expel demons in your name and do lots of miracles in your name?' Then I'll tell them, 'I've never known you. Get away from me, you people who do wrong.' "
>
> Matthew 7:21-23

Of course, parables like the Weeds and the Wheat (13:24-30) and the Net (13:47-50) compare the kingdom of heaven to end-time sifting. And when Jesus talks about a final meal where many will come from the east and the west to dine with Abraham and Isaac and Jacob in the kingdom of heaven (8:11), he is clearly talking about the future.

But Matthew also uses "kingdom of heaven" in ways that have here-and-now connotations. Jesus says the kingdom of heaven belongs to the hopeless (5:3) and the persecuted (5:10), and he does so in the present tense. He also says that the one who is least in the kingdom of heaven (now) is greater than John the Baptist (11:11). Perhaps the greatest sign that Matthew imagines the kingdom as both a present and a future reality occurs in the Lord's Prayer.

> Bring in your kingdom
> so that your will is done on earth as it's done in heaven.
>
> Matthew 6:10

This isn't the most familiar version of the prayer, but the CEB translation conveys the sentiment perfectly. God's kingdom happens when God's will is done. That can be on earth and in heaven, now or in the future.

The grace camp regards the Parable of the Workers as a story about how people enter into God's blessed future. We don't work long enough to win over God's generosity. Challenged that it seems unfair to pay the same wage to those who have worked part of the day and to those who have worked all day long under extreme conditions, the landowner replies, "Don't I have the right to do what I want with what belongs to me? Or are you resentful because I'm generous?" (20:15).

Indeed, divine generosity is good news for all of us.

Enough for Everyone: The Justice Camp and the Grace Camp

While the grace camp looks to the future, the justice camp fixes its attention on the here and now. The first group of workers bargain for a denarion for their labor, but the others are promised only "whatever is right" (20:4). This discrepancy sets up an expectation that the landowner will pay the laborers according to the amount of time they have worked. But at the end of the day, each worker receives the same wage, a single denarion.

Apparently, "whatever is right" is the same for everyone.

Readers in the justice camp primarily stress how every worker receives the basic daily wage. Where the grace camp interprets the details of the parable in spiritual terms, the justice camp won't let go of the story's roots: poor laborers who need to get paid.

We might frame the disagreement another way. The two ways of interpreting the parable agree on one key question, and they disagree on another. They agree on the nature of divine justice, but they disagree as to the relationship between a parable and its metaphors.

Both the grace camp and the justice camp agree that divine justice involves providing people what they need most. For the grace camp, what we need most is salvation, final deliverance from sin and entrance into eternal life. According to this interpretation, salvation does not depend on how much good a person has accomplished in life or how long a person has served God. Salvation depends solely upon God's goodness or grace.

When I was in seventh grade I committed an act of vandalism serious enough to get attention from the local police and the school district. I distinctly remember walking home after the act. My accomplice and I did not expect to get caught. Inside, I was rationalizing to myself; it was as if I felt like I wasn't really guilty because I was not the kind of kid who would do something so destructive. But I was guilty, and I got caught.

Justice could have worked many ways. I was a good student. I had a reputation as a nice kid. I was white. My mom taught in another school district. Someone could say I got off light in that I wasn't entered into the juvenile criminal justice system, as some other kids would have been, and I get that. One model of justice says you punish a person in proportion to the harm they have done, and I was held accountable in that way. But another model of justice says you try to make things better for everyone, to repair the harm that has occurred, to provide not what everyone has earned but what everyone needs.

This understanding of justice runs counter to the notions of justice we encounter in our daily lives. The parable recognizes this discrepancy. Those who have worked all day observe their co-workers receive the same pay they receive. We are hardly surprised when they complain: "These who were hired last worked one hour, and they received the same pay as we did even though we had to work the whole day in the hot sun" (20:12). Having taught this parable dozens of times, I can attest that many readers can relate.

When the parable began, those same workers who now complain shared a common situation with the ones who only got to work one hour. They all showed up in the same marketplace looking for work, presumably because they needed the wages. One notion of justice says their situation has changed because some workers have worked longer hours than others have. The other claims that their needs have not changed at all.

Both the grace camp and the justice camp agree on this same radical notion of justice, but they apply it in different ways. The grace camp applies it to salvation, while the justice camp attaches it to the material conditions of living. For the justice camp, the parable shows that when the kingdom of heaven is in effect, everyone gets what they need. Earlier in Matthew, John the Baptist reaches out to Jesus from prison, asking, "Are you the one who is to come, or should we look for another?" (11:3). Jesus' reply involves very present concerns.

> Go, report to John what you hear and see. Those who were blind are able to see. Those who were crippled are walking. People with skin diseases are cleansed. Those who were deaf now hear. Those who were dead are raised up. The poor have good news proclaimed to them.
>
> Matthew 11:4-5

If the two camps agree on the nature of divine justice, they disagree on how parables relate to their metaphors. We have encountered this question before. A parable draws some sort of comparison or analogy between ordinary things and the things of God. A sower goes out sowing, but the parable is really about responses to the word. How seriously, then, do agricultural details figure into our understanding of the parable?

Many of Jesus' parables go beyond the natural order into the realm of human interactions. The Parable of the Workers in the Vineyard, and all the remaining parables in this study, involve human beings. We encounter wedding parties, highway robberies, family dramas, and the inequities between the rich and the poor. Some parables feature relationships between slaveowners and enslaved persons, tenant farmers, and widows pleading their cases before corrupt judges. It's easier to set aside inanimate seeds and focus our minds on spiritual lessons, far more difficult for our imaginations to abandon workers arguing over fair wages.

Justice camp readers argue that Jesus framed his parables around such mundane human matters because issues like status, labor, and relationships were important to him. The grace camp members would respond that Jesus simply chose realities familiar to his audience in order to convey spiritual truths. Disagreements like these run deeper than simple literary theory—if we could pretend that literary theory were simple. They go to the heart of what we imagine Jesus was about. A recent Twitter flare-up reflects how divergent attitudes toward Jesus might shape our approach to the parables. The influential pastor Timothy Keller wrote,

> Jesus didn't come primarily to solve the economic, political, and social problems of the world. He came to forgive our sins. (December 18, 2017)

It didn't take long for the best-selling author Rachel Held Evans to reply.

> Maybe I misunderstand Keller, but this strikes me as a false dichotomy. Jesus spoke of both personal and systemic, societal sins. And he spoke of nothing more frequently than the Kingdom, of God's plan to achieve justice & righteousness on earth as it is in heaven. (December 19, 2017)

To be clear, Keller has written quite extensively on topics related to social justice. We won't create a false conflict between the two popular authors here. However, the brief Twitter exchange did spark a debate between Christians who emphasize Jesus' spiritual benefits and those who interpret the kingdom as a social justice movement.

Perhaps the Lord's Prayer might again provide some guidance for our reflections. We have already shown that the prayer presents God's kingdom as present wherever and whenever God's will is being done: "Bring in your kingdom so that your will is done on earth as it's done in heaven" (6:10). The next line petitions God for the ordinary needs of daily living: "Give us the bread we need for today" (6:11). Then comes the petition that confuses Christians who visit churches across denominational lines. Compare the CEB and the NRSV with the *Book of Common Prayer* of the Episcopal Church.

CEB	NRSV	Book of Common Prayer (Episcopal Church)
Forgive us for the ways we have wronged you, just as we also forgive those who have wronged us.	And forgive us our debts, as we also have forgiven our debtors.	And forgive us our trespasses, as we forgive those who trespass against us.

The CEB and the *Book of Common Prayer* translate the Greek word *opheilemata* in terms of sins or offenses: "the ways we have wronged you," or "trespasses." But the NRSV renders the same word as "debts," which is closer to its ordinary meaning. (Luke's version of the prayer asks forgiveness of *hamartia*, or "sins.") Jesus does teach his disciples to practice forgiveness, just as they receive forgiveness from God (18:15-35; 5:23-26). But does his forgiveness extend to material debt as well?

The justice camp calls attention to the workers, their needs, and their payment. They all arrive at the market early in the morning to seek work. They wait all day long because they need employment. In the end they all get what they need. "You also go into the vineyard, and I'll pay you whatever is right" (20:4).

The Group That Shall Not Be Named

A potential for ugliness lurks when this parable is discussed. An anti-Jewish note often insinuates itself into the conversation. Anti-Jewish readings of the parable have an ancient pedigree, showing themselves as well in the history of interpretation. The Christian violence against Jews provides ample caution against wicked interpretation, so we want to be well informed.

The anti-Jewish reading often builds upon the grace-oriented interpretation. It associates the workers who work all day long with Israel. According to this interpretation, they feel they have "earned" their salvation through "works righteousness." Their complaint is that newcomers—Gentile believers?—have found salvation apart from the law of Israel. In this reading, Jews resent the grace-filled good news of the law-free gospel.

This interpretation has countless problems. We'll restrict ourselves to two. First, Matthew's Gospel insists upon the value of keeping the Law and doing what Jesus says. The famous Great Commission at the end of Matthew, in which the risen Jesus commands his disciples to make disciples of the Gentiles, includes the command to teach them "to obey everything that I've commanded you" (28:20). Matthew clearly cares about obedience.

Second, anti-Jewish interpretations fundamentally misunderstand both ancient and contemporary Judaism. The concept of grace begins with God's covenant with Abraham. God reveals God's mercy to Moses on Mount Sinai:

The LORD! The LORD!
a God who is compassionate and merciful,
> very patient,
> full of great loyalty and faithfulness,
> showing great loyalty to a thousand generations,
> forgiving every kind of sin and rebellion,
> yet by no means clearing the guilty,
> punishing for their parents' sins
> their children and their grandchildren,
> as well as the third and the fourth generation.

Exodus 34:6-7

The same blend of divine mercy and justice that we find in Matthew is already present in Exodus—just as we will encounter it throughout the Psalms. It seems Christians who imagine a grace-less and works-bound Judaism must not discuss religion with and learn from their Jewish neighbors.

Jesus' Upside-Down World

Grace camp interpretations emphasize the landowner's generosity, while the justice camp stresses that each worker receives a fair wage. Both interpretations show that God's justice gives everyone what she or he needs, but they perceive human need differently. Does the parable primarily involve spiritual salvation, or does the kingdom of heaven bear upon our material conditions as well?

In my experience, very, very few readers notice what I think is the strangest aspect of the parable. Everyone notices that all the workers receive the same wage, but almost no one notices that those who work the longest are forced to stand around and watch while the newcomers receive their pay first. The instruction comes *right in the middle of the parable*: "Call the workers and give them their wages, beginning with the last ones hired and moving on finally to the first" (20:8).

This is the "hook" of the parable. For if this were to happen in the real world, it would be truly strange. Indeed, those who had begun working early in the morning would take deep offense, as if their employer were directly insulting them. It's one thing to pay everyone the same. It is entirely another thing to make them stand and watch while the newcomers receive their pay first. No wonder, as the parable goes, these workers come to expect that they will receive even more, although the landowner is happy to remind them of their earlier agreement.

Some interpreters will object that this interpretation makes too much of a small detail, the proverbial mountain out of a molehill. They could add that it is necessary for the all-day workers to watch the newcomers get paid in order for the dialogue to ensue. The parable just doesn't work without this moment.

Yet the parable's larger structure reinforces this central moment. The landowner's command to pay the last first and then move on to the first occurs in the middle of the parable. But consider the line immediately preceding the parable. Jesus has just turned away a potential disciple, a rich man who could not part with his possessions. Although it is extremely difficult for rich people to enter the kingdom, Jesus says, "all things are possible for God" (19:26). Jesus then promises that every disciple who leaves home to follow him will inherit a new family and a new home—yes, and eternal life—for "many who are first will be last. And many who are last will be first" (19:30).

There's that theme: the first last, and the last first. And it comes packaged with both hope for eternal life and concern about material possessions.

Now we consider the conclusion of the parable: "So those who are last will be first. And those who are first will be last" (20:16). The structure of the parable, including the passage that precedes it, suggests that both spiritual and material concerns are in view. But the parable's primary edge lies beyond those concerns. The parable's sharp edge lies with that "hook," a reversal in expectation. It's not simply that in God's reign everyone receives enough. It's that Jesus proclaims a world in which our assumptions about standing in God's dominion are flipped upside-down. Those who think they're first had better think again!

This message resonates with a larger pattern in Matthew in perhaps unexpected ways. Matthew's interest in final judgment imagery often packs an element of surprise. Many readers are familiar with the Parable of the Sheep and the Goats (25:31-46). We expect the goats to complain: how could they expect to know they are goats? But the sheep are no less surprised: "Lord, when did we see you hungry or thirsty or a stranger or naked or sick or in prison and didn't do anything to help you?" (25:44). Likewise, how should one set of bridesmaids know to bring extra oil, thereby being wise, while the others do not, and how does one set of enslaved laborers know to invest their coins (25:1-30)? On the final day, Jesus warns, many will say, "Lord, Lord," but Jesus will not acknowledge them (7:21-23). Matthew's Jesus does not evaluate people according to our standards.

Chapter 3

Weddings Gone Awry

The Parables of the Wedding Party and the Ten Young Bridesmaids

Jesus responded by speaking again in parables: "The kingdom of heaven is like a king who prepared a wedding party for his son. He sent his servants to call those invited to the wedding party. But they didn't want to come. Again he sent other servants and said to them, 'Tell those who have been invited, "Look, the meal is all prepared. I've butchered the oxen and the fattened cattle. Now everything's ready. Come to the wedding party!" ' But they paid no attention and went away—some to their fields, others to their businesses. The rest of them grabbed his servants, abused them, and killed them.

"The king was angry. He sent his soldiers to destroy those murderers and set their city on fire. Then he said to his servants, 'The wedding party is prepared, but those who were invited weren't worthy. Therefore, go to the roads on the edge of town and invite everyone you find to the wedding party.'

"Then those servants went to the roads and gathered everyone they found, both evil and good. The wedding party was full of guests. Now when the king came in and saw the guests, he spotted a man who wasn't wearing wedding clothes. He said to him, 'Friend, how did you get in here without wedding clothes?' But he was speechless. Then the king said to his servants, 'Tie his hands and feet and throw him out into the farthest darkness. People there will be weeping and grinding their teeth.'

"Many people are invited, but few people are chosen."

Matthew 22:1-14

"At that time the kingdom of heaven will be like ten young bridesmaids who took their lamps and went out to meet the groom. Now five of them were wise, and the other five were foolish. The foolish ones took their lamps but didn't bring oil for them. But the wise ones took their lamps and also brought containers of oil.

"When the groom was late in coming, they all became drowsy and went to sleep. But at midnight there was a cry, 'Look, the groom! Come out to meet him.'

"Then all those bridesmaids got up and prepared their lamps. But the foolish bridesmaids said to the wise ones, 'Give us some of your oil, because our lamps have gone out.'

"But the wise bridesmaids replied, 'No, because if we share with you, there won't be enough for our lamps and yours. We have a better idea. You go to those who sell oil and buy some for yourselves.' But while they were gone to buy oil, the groom came. Those who were ready went with him into the wedding. Then the door was shut.

"Later the other bridesmaids came and said, 'Lord, lord, open the door for us.'

"But he replied, 'I tell you the truth, I don't know you.'

"Therefore, keep alert, because you don't know the day or the hour."

Matthew 25:1-13

In this chapter we discuss two parables rather than one, the parables of the Wedding Party (Matthew 22:1-14) and the Ten Young Bridesmaids (25:1-13). We've already mentioned both parables in passing. The Parable of the Ten Young Bridesmaids occurs only in Matthew, while the Wedding Party has a close parallel in Luke (14:16-24). We'll devote our attention only to Matthew's version of the Wedding Party, noting how it differs from Luke's parable but focusing on the distinctive way Matthew tells the story.

Multiple Versions of the Same Parable?

Several of Jesus' parables appear in multiple Gospels. No two commentators agree on exactly the same list, but of nearly forty parables, we find nine or ten in two or more of the Gospels. Never do two accounts of the same parable agree word for word. Why?

The primary explanation involves how the Gospels were written. Most scholars regard Mark as the earliest of the Gospels, with Matthew and Luke using copies of Mark as the backbone for their own stories. It seems Matthew and Luke shared some other material as well.

Where Matthew and Luke differ from Mark, or from one another, sometimes the differences involve simple literary style. Just as often the differences are thematic or theological. We've already seen that Matthew is fond of judgment imagery. Luke has a tendency to add explanations to the parables: "Jesus was telling them a parable about their need to pray continuously and not to be discouraged" (18:1).

We consider these two parables together for several reasons. First, they both involve weddings where something goes very wrong. Second, there's an element of judgment or exclusion. Third, the parables occur in a section of Matthew filled with eschatological themes and judgment imagery. Matthew 24 provides Matthew's version of the "little apocalypse," the extended speech in which Jesus discusses the coming of the Son of Man, the fall of Jerusalem, a period of false messiahs and prophets and of distressing signs in the skies. Matthew 25 follows with the parables of the Bridesmaids, the Valuable Coins (or Talents), and the Sheep and the Goats, all involving judgment imagery. We can read these judgment themes all the way back, past the Parable of the Wedding Party to Matthew 21:33. However we decide to interpret Matthew's story line, once Jesus shows up in Jerusalem in chapter 21, conflict begins to intensify, and Jesus' teaching turns toward themes of judgment. Both the Wedding Party and Bridesmaids parables appear in this section of Matthew.

The Wedding Party: From Odd to Bizarre

We can't say the Parable of the Wedding Party gets off to an ordinary beginning. A royal wedding is hardly ordinary, but such things do happen. And while modern readers may find it curious that the king issues two invitations to the wedding guests, ancient hearers would not have found that remarkable at all. The first invitation tells people on what date to come to the wedding—"save the date"—while a second comes on the day of the party announcing that it is time to arrive. "Look, the meal is all prepared. I've butchered the oxen and the fattened cattle. Now everything's ready. Come to the wedding party!" (22:4).

Nothing to see here. Yet.

When we read a parable, we expect to abandon the ordinary. I'm not into celebrities, nor do I follow royalty, but I'd almost surely accept an invitation to a royal wedding. Imagine people who would turn down an invitation from their own king! We're talking about more than missing out on the event of the year. We're talking about offending someone who can make your life miserable, or worse.

Let's remember the key point. These wedding guests have already accepted their initial invitations. When Jesus says, "They paid no attention and went away—some to their fields, others to their businesses" (22:5), he is describing not indifference but a direct insult. The Greek is more direct: they neglected, or ignored, the call to come to the party. Things have regressed from an extraordinary party to a sharp conflict. Things have gone wrong.

When we read parables, we look for a hook, that moment when the story abandons the realm of the ordinary and, as C. H. Dodd once said, "[arrests] the hearer by its vividness or strangeness."[1] This parable has hardly gotten started.

Matthew adds this detail: "The rest of them grabbed his servants, abused them, and killed them" (22:6). We have abandoned the realm of the strange for an expedition into the truly bizarre. Surely these guests know that whoever assaults the king's enslaved servants has effectively insulted the king. Who would do that?

The king responds in two ways, one predictable and one not so predictable. The predictable response is to repay violence with violence. The king "destroys" the rebellious subjects and burns their city. This detail returns us to the problem of Matthew's relationship to Judaism. The Parable of the Tenant Farmers (21:33-46) immediately precedes the Wedding Party, and Jesus directs it against the chief

38

priests and the Pharisees (21:45). The wicked tenants behave very much like the initial wedding invitees, abusing the landowner's enslaved workers and then killing his son. The landowner destroys those tenants and rents the vineyard to others, just as the king destroys the wedding invitees and invites still other guests. The two parables use the same Greek word meaning to destroy—it can also mean to kill—in case we might miss the point.

To drive this point home, Jesus tells the priests and Pharisees: "I tell you that God's kingdom will be taken away from you and will be given to a people who produce its fruit" (21:43). This sounds very much like a theology in which God's favor moves away from Israel to embrace Gentiles. The close relationship between the parables of the Wedding Party and the Tenant Farmers gives us reason for concern. The king's violence is predictable, but it is also distressing.

The king's second action is more surprising. He invites a whole new crowd to the party, presumably those considered unworthy of an initial invitation. Indeed, the enslaved workers collect "both evil and good" guests without discrimination. And the hall is full of guests.

Once again, we encounter Matthew's theme of eschatological surprise. Eschatology has to do with ultimate things, issues like the ultimate course of history or what lies beyond death. When we discussed the Parable of the Workers in the Vineyard, we reflected on Matthew's judgment scenes, when characters often experience surprise. The classic example is the Parable of the Sheep and the Goats (25:31-46). The goats protest upon learning their goatly identity, and we expect that, but the sheep are no less surprised. Now we have wedding guests who started the day having no idea it would turn out anything but ordinary. Now they're in the hall of a royal wedding.

Another Matthean parable uses imagery of the "good and the bad" mixed together, though with different Greek wording. (Depending on the English translation you use, this can be hard to notice.) In the Parable of the Net (13:47-50), Jesus describes a catch of fish, both "good" and "rotten" gathered together and then sorted. At the end of the age, Jesus says, the angels throw away "the evil ones"—this is the same word we encounter in 22:10—into a burning furnace, where people will weep and grind their teeth. Remarkably, at the wedding party the good and the bad (wicked) all celebrate together.

A Double Surprise: The "Other" Guest

Compared with Luke's version of the Wedding Party parable, Matthew's first additional element involves the violence exchanged between the invitees and the king, all the more shocking because the host is the king and not simply a "certain someone," as it is in Luke. Matthew includes a second major additional factor, the solitary wedding guest who lacks a proper wedding garment (22:11-14). This unfortunate guest winds up cast into the outer darkness bound hand and foot—yes, with the weeping and teeth gnashing.

At the risk of over-interpretation, we might observe the obvious. This poor guest was better off before he ever received an invitation. Now that he's been invited, his failure to wear festive garments seals his fate. Better to have gone out of town on business. Matthew's element of surprise strikes again.

This part of the story raises a question that may well be unanswerable: is it fair to hold this man accountable for not wearing a wedding garment?

On the side of accountability, let's observe that this guest alone is singled out. The parable describes the king looking over the guests, all of whom apparently pass his inspection. Some interpreters insist that the second set of wedding guests have had time to go home and change, an impression strengthened by the contrast between them and the poor schmuck who gets cast out from the party. We also have no evidence that most ancient people possessed "wedding garments." Perhaps, then, all that is expected is for the man to go home and put on his most decent—or clean—clothes.

But there's something to be said for a certain randomness in the poor man's fate. The story does not specifically say that the second round of guests received time to change clothes. On the contrary, the enslaved workers are said to have "gathered" all the guests. This is a small detail, but it's not the same as saying they had simply issued invitations. Had the guests received invitations, they would have time to respond, including cleaning, changing, or borrowing clothes. On the contrary, the story gives the impression they all arrive at once.

It's impossible to be certain whether the man should or should not have arrived prepared for a wedding. This seems to be an important question. I think the reasons to regard him as accountable for having failed to dress appropriately may weigh more heavily than the reasons to regard his judgment as arbitrary, but I'm far from confident in this judgment.

The Wedding Party: Far from Secure

Everything about the Parable of the Wedding Party counsels against a false sense of security. The initial group of invitees for some reason chooses to insult the king, disregard his invitation, and do violence to his enslaved workers. Perhaps they function as stand-ins for Jesus' enemies, the temple authorities and Pharisees, against whom Jesus is arguing in the preceding parable, the Tenant Farmers (21:33-46). Nevertheless, the notion that even the initial invitees find themselves excluded from the celebration, even *replaced*, is unsettling.

The second group of partygoers looks more promising. It includes the worthy and the unworthy, all gathered by the king's representatives without distinction. But one guest finds himself singled out for his lack of preparation, and for him grace has run out. No one offers him an extra garment. Instead, he finds himself in the outer darkness, bound hand and foot. Perhaps he would have been better off having received no invitation at all.

One option would be to divide the parable into its two movements, separating them into two fundamentally alienated parts. The end result would have us favoring one section over the other, as many interpreters do. The first part, 22:1-10, ends with a hall filled with guests, a sharp contrast with the "few are chosen" of 22:11-14. The first part moves from people who take their invitations for granted to the joyous vision of a party populated by people who never expected to attend a royal wedding, while the second part sets its focus upon a man tossed out from that festive moment.

To pick and choose according to our preferences might be convenient, but it would also neglect the ways in which this whole unit fits into Matthew's larger literary design. For Matthew is a Gospel of surprise and insecurity. "Many people are invited," Jesus concludes, "but few people are chosen" (22:14). What does that even mean? How does it make sense to *invite* many but to *choose* few? And what does that mean for us listeners?

Bridesmaids and an Oil Scarcity (25:1-13)

Matthew's second wedding parable relies upon the motif of delay. Again, the parable begins, "The kingdom of heaven is like . . ." But this time the kingdom is not like a king but like ten young bridesmaids.

Let's begin with the setup. Ten young women are bridesmaids, or virgins in Greek. We're to imagine wedding attendants, all quite young women, perhaps even pre-teens. Their task, it seems, is to greet the groom as he enters the village for the wedding. We wish we knew more about ancient weddings. We don't know exactly what these young women are supposed to be doing or how their role relates to the wedding. The presence of ten bridesmaids suggests a large wedding. So perhaps we are to imagine a fairly large wedding procession, where the young women are to present initial greetings to the bridegroom and his party. If so, their role would be significant.

The Kingdom Metaphor

Many theologians and pastors suggest that contemporary Christians should move beyond the "kingdom of God" and "kingdom of heaven" metaphors. For one thing, kings rule by domination and the threat of force. Contemporary Christians emphasize that God works not by threatening to harm us but through the power of love. Indeed, most modern societies now regard monarchy and dictatorship as inferior forms of governance precisely because they rely on compulsion rather than upon the popular will. There's also the matter of gender. Like the popular movie *The Lion King*, kingdom of God imagery suggests that everything will be all right as long as the right *man* is ruling upon the big rock. Is God limited to one gender-specific mode of being? If so, what do we make of Genesis 1:27, in which all of humankind, whatever gender, are created in the divine image? Kingdom metaphors also suggest a realm or territory, as if God's influence is confined by boundaries.

All these problems are real, and they suggest that kingdom language has limited value for our use in worship and devotional life. Some liturgical (worship) theologians have suggested alternative language like the *kin-dom of God*, for example. Whatever we decide regarding our worship life, I would suggest we remember the political power of the kingdom metaphor in its ancient context. Ancient Jews and Christians referred to God as a king or a judge because they

---

knew what how corrupt and violent human judges and kings could be. They far preferred the image of a ruler who reigns with compassion and fairness.

Right away we're told that five of the young women are wise and five are foolish. There are only two species of bridesmaids, differentiated by one factor. It doesn't matter if they do their homework, attend to their health, or cultivate the skills expected of young Galilean women. Whether they are wise or foolish depends on whether they remember to bring oil. As readers, we will encounter no surprise in this parable: we know what factor will determine the outcome of the story.

But the wording of the story will cause confusion: "The foolish ones took their lamps but didn't bring oil for them. But the wise ones took their lamps and also brought containers of oil" (25:3-4).

Simply from reading the story, we'd get the impression that one group brought lamps without oil while the other brought lamps with oil. That's not how the story plays out. In verse 8, we find that the "foolish" bridesmaids have run out of oil. In other words, they brought their lamps along with the oil their lamps contained, but the wise bridesmaids brought vessels of extra oil. They were prepared for a delay.

The parable turns around two factors, the distinction between the bridesmaids who bring extra oil and those who don't and the delay of the bridegroom. Apart from this parable, the term *bridegroom* ("groom" in the CEB) occurs only one other time in Matthew. The disciples of John the Baptist observe that they, like the Pharisees, fast often. But Jesus' disciples do not fast at all. Jesus replies: "The wedding guests can't mourn while the groom is still with them, can they? But the days will come when the groom will be taken away from them, and then they'll fast" (9:14-15).

Jesus' reply proves significant for our parable for a couple of reasons. First, Jesus identifies himself with the term "groom." Jesus is, well, the life of the party. We recall that the apostle Paul will use the metaphor of marriage to describe the church (2 Corinthians 11:2; Ephesians 5:25-32), and the book of Revelation picks up on this theme in a major way (Revelation 19:6-9; 21:2).

The association with Revelation brings out the second connection between Matthew 9:14-15 and the Parable of the Bridesmaids: both passages involve eschatology, matters having to do with our ultimate hope. In Matthew 9, Jesus is saying that his disciples don't have the need to fast like John's disciples and the Pharisees do because Jesus' disciples know they're living in the messianic age: the bridegroom is among them. So, Jesus goes on, a time will come when the bridegroom is absent. And then the disciples will need to fast again (9:15).

The Parable of the Bridesmaids is apparently speaking to that time when the bridegroom is absent, the period between Jesus' departure and his return. Biblical scholars use a fancy term for this period: "the delay of the Parousia." *Parousia* simply means "arrival," and in this context it refers to Jesus' glorious arrival to make things finally right in the world. The bridesmaids need extra oil because they should prepare for a long period of waiting and readiness.

The Delay of the Parousia

Reflective Christians have long struggled with the question of Jesus' return. The earliest Christian writings available to us are not the Gospels but the letters of Paul. In his earlier writings Paul expects Jesus to return in his lifetime. In 1 Thessalonians he refers to "we who are alive and still around at the Lord's coming" (4:15). Discussing Jesus' return in 1 Corinthians, he attests, "All of us won't die, but we will all be changed" (15:51). As time passes, it seems Paul opens himself to the possibility that his life might come to a close before Jesus returns (Philippians 1:20-26).

The Gospels themselves reflect this tension. Speaking of the end times, Jesus tells his disciples "this generation won't pass away until all these things happen" (Matthew 24:34; Mark 13:30; Luke 21:32 paraphrase). But several of Matthew's parables also feature a waiting motif, in which an authority figure departs on a journey, with judgment coming upon his return. These include the Tenant Farmers (21:33-46), the Faithful and Unfaithful Servants (24:45-51), and the Valuable Coins (25:14-30).

The delay of the bridegroom and the bridesmaids' need for extra oil are allegorical elements in the parable. All parables feature an element of comparison: somehow aspects of the parable draw us to imagine things differently. The Parable of the Bridesmaids begins,

"The kingdom of heaven is like," inviting us to check our assumptions about how God is active in the world. But not all parables are allegorical, with some or all of their key elements corresponding directly to specific other realities. The Parable of the Sower and the Soils is an allegory: the seed corresponds to the message of the kingdom, while the soils indicate diverse responses to that message. But the Parable of the Workers in the Vineyard does not seem particularly allegorical: nothing in that story teaches about exactly some other thing in particular. Here the bridegroom's delay reminds us of believers awaiting Jesus' return, which could happen at any moment—and could take a very long time. The bridesmaids' need for oil is a bit more vague, but it indicates a certain kind of preparedness. I grew up in small-town Alabama, where my older male relatives all carried pocketknives—you know, just in case something needed cutting. A kid would get expelled for carrying a knife to school these days, but I did so many days.

No Hook at All?

I have suggested that Jesus' parables generally have a "hook," that moment where a story abandons ordinary logic and things jump off the rails. The Workers in the Vineyard parable has a double hook: not only do all the workers receive the same wage, the ones who worked longest must stand around and watch while those who worked the least receive their wages first. Allegorical parables are less likely to have a dramatic hook, as the logic of allegory needs to work smoothly; however, we explored the mystery of a sower who scatters seed on unpromising soil.

The Parable of the Bridesmaids begins as if it will have no strange moment. From the very beginning we know there will be wise and foolish bridesmaids, and we know the issue that divides them will involve bringing extra oil. The metaphor of a late bridegroom sets up the conflict that will reveal their relative wisdom and foolishness. Perhaps this parable will have no suspense at all, no provocation "to tease the mind into active thought," as C. H. Dodd would have said.[2]

In this respect, we might compare the Parable of the Bridesmaids with another of Jesus' parables, that of the Two Foundations. Matthew's great Sermon on the Mount encompasses three chapters and provides the Gospel's introduction to Jesus' teaching for would-be disciples (chapters 5-7). At the sermon's conclusion, Jesus admonishes his audience: "Not everybody who says to me, 'Lord, Lord,' will get into the kingdom of heaven. Only those who do the will of my Father who is in heaven will enter" (7:21).

This is Matthew's unique emphasis: to follow Jesus is to do as Jesus teaches. It's that straightforward. Jesus then lays out the Parable of the Two Foundations (7:24-27; see Luke 6:47-49), the Gospel's equivalent of the Three Little Pigs. One who hears and does what Jesus teaches is like a person who builds upon rock; one who hears and does not observe Jesus' teaching is like a person who builds upon sand. The first person's house can withstand rain, flood, and wind, while the second person's house will face disaster. The Two Foundations parable is a fairly simple allegorical illustration, not unlike the Bridesmaids.

Or so it seems. As we've seen before, a lot depends on how far we're willing to push the details of a parable. Imagine we're among the ten bridesmaids. We all have our lamps, and we're waiting for the groom. Perhaps we've kept our lamps trimmed and burning, as the old gospel song goes. That song is often attributed to the great singer Blind Willie Johnson, but surely he picked up on a version he encountered in church. At some point we realize the groom is delayed.

Now we all have decisions to make. If five of us bridesmaids are so wise, wouldn't *one* of us suggest that one or two keep their lamps burning while the rest conserve our oil? To put it differently, might not a truer wisdom open that path to cooperation as opposed to the parable's winner-takes-all mentality? The parable seems to define wisdom in terms of having—and keeping—enough for oneself and ignoring everyone else.

Some readers identify this problem, the unnecessary division among the bridesmaids when other and better ways are possible, as the parable's hook. Others counter that this sort of logic abuses the parable. It jumps outside the world of the parable, twisting it beyond recognition. Parables, they would say, build points of comparison between their story world and the ways of God. They're not meant to account for civil engineering, game theory, or group problem solving. They're simply designed to open people's minds about the things of God.

Furthermore, perhaps Matthew—and perhaps Jesus—advanced a certain zero-sum logic. In the very next parable, the Parable of the Valuable Coins, Jesus sets forth this principle: "Those who have much will receive more, and they will have more than they need. But as for those who don't have much, even the little bit they have will be taken away from them" (25:29; see Luke 19:26).

Indeed, Matthew's Jesus appeals to the same logic in explaining his use of parables: "For those who have will receive more and they will have more than enough. But as for those who don't have, even the little they have will be taken away from them" (13:12).

We modern readers don't much care for such logic. It seems unfair that the haves get more and the have-nots lose out. But neither Matthew nor Jesus necessarily conforms to our sense of fairness.

That kind of absolute thinking defines this parable, provoking some readers to reflect. Is it truly God's way to divide humanity into two categories, the wise and the foolish, based upon whether they discern the need for long-term preparation? Or is the parable designed to make its hearers uncomfortable precisely at that point, provoking us to examine our own wisdom and our own preparation?

Fortunately for the unprepared bridesmaids, there's no outer darkness with weeping and gnashing of teeth. But they do miss out on the wedding party. The parable's language slides from a focus upon the bridegroom to words we've heard earlier in Matthew's story: "Lord, lord, open the door for us" (25:11). We're not talking about the bridegroom anymore, are we? We're talking about the Lord Jesus.

Uh-oh. We heard, "Lord, Lord," back in chapter 7, at the end of the Sermon on the Mount (7:21-23). In fact, we've already mentioned it a couple of times. It wasn't good. Not everyone who calls Jesus "Lord, Lord," enters the realm of heaven. Here in the Parable of the Bridesmaids Jesus nearly repeats himself from chapter 7: "I tell you the truth, I don't know you" (25:12).

Two Weddings, Two Parties, Two Sets of Closed Doors

When ancient Jews and Christians went looking for metaphors that conveyed the boundless joy of living in the fullness of God's joy, weddings and parties climbed near the top of their lists. Weddings and the parties that go with them are cause for great celebration: they hold the promise of youth, of lives opening to the world, of families coming together and growing, and of love finding its way in the world. In the Parable of the Wedding Party, the king is so deeply committed to celebrating that he invites everyone he can find until the party is full! Likewise, in the Parable of the Bridesmaids, we can imagine these young women eager to escort the bridegroom to the party until they grow heavy with sleep—and then the shout: "Look, the groom!" (25:6).

I write this having celebrated just my second anniversary—of my second wedding. My wife and I blended our families: four children, a grandson. We chose to invite only a small group of family and friends, worship God, enjoy good food and drink, dance to fun music, and celebrate the people who love and support us. I'm smiling right now as I type, and the anniversary was just six days ago.

Literature and film are replete with other weddings, sad weddings. Weddings of compulsion, weddings of remorse—because life can be that way. I can't stand gory movies or television, so I've never seen the "Red Wedding" episode of *Game of Thrones*, where one royal household uses a wedding as a pretext to slaughter another, but weddings offer the perfect setting for betrayal, revenge, and disappointment.

Matthew shows us two wedding parties. Each wedding party includes the joy and wonder that accompany the kingdom of heaven. Each party invites us to marvel at the possibility that we might find ourselves included, to ponder the social event of our lives, to soak in one of the most glorious images the Gospel has to offer: celebration in the presence of Jesus. Each party also confronts us with the real possibility of exclusion. Each challenges its hearers to examine themselves, ourselves, as to whether we take our status for granted, whether we prepare appropriately, and whether we remain ready even when ordinary time seems to drag on.

Chapter 4

Lawyers and Samaritans

The Parable of the Good Samaritan

A legal expert stood up to test Jesus. "Teacher," he said, "what must I do to gain eternal life?"

Jesus replied, "What is written in the Law? How do you interpret it?"

He responded, "You must love the Lord your God with all your heart, with all your being, with all your strength, and with all your mind, and love your neighbor as yourself."

Jesus said to him, "You have answered correctly. Do this and you will live."

But the legal expert wanted to prove that he was right, so he said to Jesus, "And who is my neighbor?"

Jesus replied, "A man went down from Jerusalem to Jericho. He encountered thieves, who stripped him naked, beat him up, and left him near death. Now it just so happened that a priest was also going down the same road. When he saw the injured man, he crossed over to the other side of the road and went on his way. Likewise, a Levite came by that spot, saw the injured man, and crossed over to the other side of the road and went on his way. A Samaritan, who was on a journey, came to where the man was. But when he saw him, he was moved with compassion. The Samaritan went to him and bandaged his wounds, tending them with oil and wine.

Then he placed the wounded man on his own donkey, took
him to an inn, and took care of him. The next day, he took two
full days' worth of wages and gave them to the innkeeper.
He said, 'Take care of him, and when I return, I will pay you
back for any additional costs.' What do you think? Which one
of these three was a neighbor to the man who encountered
thieves?"

Then the legal expert said, "The one who demonstrated
mercy toward him."

Jesus told him, "Go and do likewise."

Luke 10:25-37

In August 1997, Princess Diana of Wales died from injuries sustained in a high-speed car crash in Paris. Because of her massive popularity, her death brought about waves of public grief accompanied by blanketing media coverage. The tragic nature of the accident—her car was racing to avoid tabloid photographers—only fueled the public outcry. For weeks the only news story to rival Diana's death was the death of Mother Teresa on September 5, the two having forged a remarkable friendship. Only later would the public come to appreciate how the two women, so very different in lifestyle and outward appearance, shared a profound common loneliness.

The days following Princess Diana's death introduced many of us to a new legal concept: the "Good Samaritan laws." In French law, failure to provide aid to someone in danger is a crime, with possible penalties including multiyear prison sentences and large fines. Conversely, Good Samaritan laws do protect people from legal liability when they are engaged in good-faith efforts to rescue others from danger. If I break your car window in an attempt to rescue you, Good Samaritan laws exempt me from liability for the cost of the repair.

Good Samaritan laws reflect the New Testament's most famous parable and its most common interpretation: Jesus meant for his followers to help people in need. Human beings naturally want to set up boundaries: how widely does the circle of obligation extend? Good Samaritan laws recognize no such boundaries. Unless rescuing someone puts our own lives in danger or endangers the lives of others, we are obliged to help. The Good Samaritan's example smashes the boundaries that divide people from one another. Even our enemies merit our help.

Flipping the Script

An alternative reading of the Parable of the Good Samaritan (Luke 10:25-37) emerged during the civil rights era. It may have a much older pedigree. This interpretation started in the black preaching tradition and then was appropriated by progressive white preachers who wanted their congregations to honor the humanity of their African American neighbors. According to this interpretation, the Samaritan corresponds to a black person in the United States during the time of segregation. (Although it was practiced differently in different parts of the country, segregation was scarcely limited to the South.) One classic rendition of this interpretation appears in Clarence Jordan's *The Cotton Patch Version of Luke and Acts*, a free translation of those biblical books into colloquial Southern vernacular.[1]

> A man was going from Atlanta to Albany and some gangsters held him up. When they had robbed him of his wallet and brand-new suit, they beat him up and drove off in his car, leaving him unconscious by the shoulder of the highway.
>
> Now it just so happened that a white preacher was going down that same highway. When he saw the fellow, he stepped on the gas and went scooting by.
>
> Shortly afterwards a white Gospel song leader came down the road, and when he saw what had happened, he too stepped on the gas.
>
> Then a black man traveling that way came upon the fellow, and what he saw moved him to tears. He stopped and bound up his wounds as best he could, drew some water from his water-jug to wipe away the blood and then laid him on the back seat. He drove on to Albany and took him to the hospital and said to the nurse, "You all take good care of this white man I found on the highway. Here's the only two dollars I got, but you all keep account of what he owes, and if he can't pay it, I'll settle up with you when I make a pay-day."

The great innovation of this racially coded interpretation is that it focuses upon the agency of the helper rather than upon the need of the victim. The more common interpretation emphasizes our obligation to help, but this interpretation from the black preaching tradition lands upon the one who does the helping. And isn't that where Jesus' lands after telling the parable?

"What do you think? Which one of these three was a neighbor to the man who encountered thieves?" (10:36).

The Stakes

Over the years, I've grown convinced that our standard interpretation of the Good Samaritan parable is dangerous. That's not an exaggeration. Dangerous.

Obviously, it's a good thing to expand our circle of care, indeed to destroy all the boundaries that place some people outside our moral vision. Just as surely, a great deal of good has been done at the inspiration of the Good Samaritan parable. So, someone might well ask, isn't it going a bit far to write off the most common interpretation as dangerous?

Let's step back. Who's served by the common interpretation? Whose point of view does it represent? From here on out, we can start calling the "common" interpretation the "charitable" one. The charitable interpretation assumes a reader who is in a position to help, someone who can offer charity.

When we find ourselves asking how far our circle of obligation extends, our imaginations reside in a position of privilege. Taking up the charitable interpretation, we certainly do not imagine ourselves as the ones in need. We perceive ourselves only as the ones who can offer aid. For us, it's entirely optional to help other people. We *want* to do it. We will *choose* to do it. But there's a *boundary* as to how much charity we can extend. We can't expend all our resources, all our time, all our energy helping other people. We know we should love our neighbors, but we can only help so many neighbors in one lifetime. So we want to know how far our obligation extends.

With the legal expert in Luke's story, we ask, "And who is my neighbor?"

We should ask ourselves whether we want to read Jesus' parables from such a position of privilege. For one thing, life rarely plays out so dependably. We may spend most of our lives in security and self-sufficiency. How stunning it is, then, when we find ourselves in crisis, truly dependent upon the goodness of others. Many of us are poorly prepared for a time like that, whether it happens in a moment, whether it represents a temporary stage in our lives, or whether it marks a new period in our lives that we may never move through. Eventually most of us will face a time when we will seek a neighbor to help *us*, not the other way around.

There's also the problem of Jesus, who seems to prefer disciples who don't feel so secure in themselves. This is particularly the case in Luke, where insecurity abounds. The Gospel of Luke is a story of reversal. In Luke, security comes with its own flashing caution light. Having learned that she has conceived a most special child, the Son of the Most High, Mary visits her relative Elizabeth. Mary breaks out in praise, including the memorable lines:

> He has pulled the powerful down from their thrones
> and lifted up the lowly.
> He has filled the hungry with good things
> and sent the rich away empty-handed. (1:52-53)

So it is with Luke, in which Jesus announces his own mission with the prophet Isaiah's words:

> . . . to preach good news to the poor,
> to proclaim release to the prisoners
> and recovery of sight to the blind,
> to liberate the oppressed,
> and to proclaim the year of the Lord's favor.
>   Luke 4:18-19, quoting Isaiah 61:1-2 and 58:6

Luke is especially fond of what some call *crisis* parables. As the parable opens, we meet a character in a state of security. A moment of crisis arrives suddenly. In some cases, the character has an opportunity to adapt. For example, the prodigal son returns to his father (15:11-32), the dishonest manager concocts a scheme that will keep him off the streets (16:1-13), and the dishonest judge caves in to the persistent widow (18:1-8). Other characters, like the rich fool (12:15-21) and the rich man who ignores Lazarus (16:19-31), are less fortunate. They receive no second chances.

Luke's Unique Parables

Compared to Matthew and Mark, Luke contains a great deal of independent material, about half the contents of the Gospel. A good chunk of that material consists of parables, including some of the most familiar material in the entire New Testament: the Good Samaritan (10:25-37), the Prodigal Son (15:11-32), the Dishonest Manager (16:1-13), the Rich Man and Lazarus (16:19-31), the Widow and the Judge (18:1-8), and the Pharisee and the Tax Collector (18:9-14), along with about six other unique parables.

Two literary techniques distinguish Luke's parables. One is interior monologue, where the readers "overhear" what characters think to themselves. We observe the prodigal coming to his senses and planning to appeal to his father's mercy (15:17-19). There's the rich fool, telling himself he has enough to "Eat, drink, and enjoy yourself" (12:19). And we enjoy the scoundrel manager who, once turned out of his place of employment, realizes he's too weak for manual labor and too proud to beg (16:3).

The second technique applies to the Good Samaritan parable. Luke is fond of parables of crisis, stories in which a character starts off comfortably but comes to a moment of dire need. The rich fool thinks he has a long life of pleasure, but death takes him by surprise (12:15-21). The same happens to the rich man who ignores poor Lazarus (16:19-21). The prodigal son thinks he's wealthy until he's squandered everything, and his older brother thinks he's good until he finds himself uninvited to his own brother's party (15:11-32). The dishonest manager is riding high until his mismanagement is reported (16:1-13), and the dishonest judge would be just fine if that blasted widow would stop hounding him (18:1-8). The Parable of the Good Samaritan begins with a man on a journey. Travel was always dangerous in the ancient world. However, this man, presumably Jewish like Jesus and his hearers, has no idea his life will turn upon the mercy of a Samaritan, the Judeans' notorious enemy. As the commercial says, life comes at you fast in Luke.

A great deal of good has been accomplished under the banner of the Good Samaritan, who so often serves as our example when we perform acts of mercy. However, when we interpret the parable as a call to extend the boundaries of our charity, we place ourselves in a perilous position. We assume the chair of privilege, assuming we are the ones who will decide whether to extend help or not. Over and over again, Luke shows us what a dangerous seat that is to take. What if we find ourselves traveling down a road, beset by violent criminals and in desperate need of help? Will we be so selective about our neighbors then?

Neighbors, Really?

Imagine a prosperous downtown church that serves breakfast on Sunday mornings. Churches are generally very good at providing services to the poor during the week. Because of churches, the city in which I live provides three warm meals seven days a week. As the popular sociologist and preacher Tony Campolo continually reminds audiences, it's easy to criticize Christians, but a lot fewer people would be housed and fed without them. Just the same, not many well-off churches are willing to open their space to the poor on Sunday mornings. For several years I served on the staff of a church that did.

Serving breakfast required a great amount of energy—not only for the cooking but for the kitchen and dining hall setup. Right after breakfast the dining hall hosted a worship service, complete with sacraments, for the breakfast fellowship and anyone else who wanted to attend. After that service, adult education happened in the same space, requiring a quick turnaround. Poor people very close to living on the streets mingled and shared restrooms with people in nice dresses and suits while the transition went on. It was a wonderful ministry. And sometimes it was uncomfortable for both the long-time church members and for folks who came for the breakfast.

At one point an idea reached the church governing board and staff: perhaps we should hire armed security. On occasion a breakfast guest would behave in ways that were disturbing. No one questioned whether we should continue with breakfast, but folks were concerned that all people needed to be assured of their safety. When you hire armed security to watch over one group of people, what does that say about who is *us* and who is *them*? Does the presence of armed security indicate that some people are class-A neighbors and other people are another class of neighbors?

Does the question, "Who is my neighbor?" reflect an assumption of status among neighbors?

Perspective in the Parable

The Parable of the Good Samaritan begins not with the Samaritan but, as several of Luke's parables do, with "a certain man" (10:30, literal translation). This generic character invites us to identify with this man and his plight.

Ordinarily we associate anonymity with insignificance. If a character has no name, we might assume that she or he must not be important. However, anonymity has its advantages. It allows hearers to imagine ourselves in that character's place. Anonymity places no obstacles between the reader and that character.

Almost all the characters in Jesus' parables are men, a reality we tend to overlook. Historically, the absence of female characters has not prevented women from loving the parables, although women have also shown special affinity for stories with female characters. In Luke, the story of Mary and Martha has drawn a great deal of conversation among female readers. Mary the mother of Jesus does so too. The Parable of the Good Samaritan, of course, features only male characters, which is the more common case. Will readers and hearers experience the parable alongside one of the characters within this story as well?

When we reflect upon the audience of Jesus' parables, we want to be specific.

- There are the people Jesus himself addressed. In Luke's story world they are, with very few exceptions, Galileans and Judeans. The Parable of the Good Samaritan addresses a Jewish audience, occurring as Jesus is on his way to Jerusalem. He addresses the parable directly to a "legal expert," a person who understands the religious and social law of Judaism, the Torah, and to the people gathered around, including his disciples.
- There's also the audience of Luke's Gospel, the people who would have read and heard the Gospel decades after the career of Jesus. We can guess things about them. Many assume Luke was writing to non-Jews, or Gentiles, but even that conclusion is a guess. There's not much we can know about that audience except that they lived in the ancient Mediterranean world and understood Greek.

- At a third level, we're talking about ourselves, today's readers of Luke's story.

The "certain man" in our parable has no distinguishing characteristics apart from the fact that he is travelling. The other characters do. Readers and hearers would be unlikely to see themselves in either a priest or a Levite—unless they were actual priests and Levites, of course. Very few hearers or readers of this parable, whether ancient or modern, would have any reason to identify with the priest, the Levite, the Samaritan, or the innkeeper.

These reflections place Jesus' story in a certain perspective. Our most common interpretation devotes its attention to the Samaritan. Indeed, the parable gives him a lot of attention. Unlike the other characters, who say nothing and do almost nothing, the story's focus rests upon the Samaritan for a long time. We learn how he feels, "moved with compassion" (10:33). We even hear him speak. Clearly, the Samaritan is meant to draw our attention. At the end of the parable, Jesus invites the legal expert to contemplate the Samaritan: "What do you think? Which one of these three was a neighbor to the man who encountered thieves?" (10:36).

But before the Samaritan enters the story, the spotlight rests upon the anonymous man who sets off for Jericho. We meet him at the beginning, and he is the only character who is present throughout the story. If we could imagine our first encounter with the parable, before anyone ever gave it a name, would we not wonder how this man will be rescued? Once the priest has passed by, and the Levite, too, we might be ready for a surprise. That's how stories often work, especially three-step stories. The surprise comes in step three. But our chief concern will rest with the man's salvation: who will come to his rescue?

The Samaritan provides the answer to that question.

The parable's perspective leads us away from the perspective of privilege (the one who will save him) and into the position of vulnerability (the one who needs saving). And that is important.

Samaritans and Jews

Everyone who's been in church long enough knows that Samaritans and Jews are supposed to be enemies. Jesus deals with Samaritans only in the Gospels of Luke and John. In Luke, Jesus wants to visit a Samaritan village but is rejected (9:52-56); he later heals a Samaritan (17:11-19). John gives us the famous story in which Jesus meets the woman at the well. Her famous question reflects the enmity that defines the relationship between Jews and Samaritans: "Why do you, a Jewish man, ask for something to drink from me, a Samaritan woman?" John's narrator pauses to explain: "Jews and Samaritans didn't associate with each other" (4:9). But why the animosity?

After Solomon's reign, Israel divided into two kingdoms, a southern kingdom based in Jerusalem and a northern kingdom with its capital in Samaria. The Assyrians overran Samaria in 722 BCE, resulting in massive repopulation. From that period on, "Jews"—that is, those who considered themselves descendants from the southern kingdom of Judah—regarded the Samaritans as ethnically and religiously questionable. Then and even today, Samaritan worship resembled Jewish worship, but with different versions of the Torah, different places of worship, and somewhat conflicting beliefs and practices. Enmity occasionally led to violence. Jesus' choice of a Samaritan for the hero of his story is therefore intentionally provocative.

Context and Crafting

The Parable of the Good Samaritan occurs in the middle of a conversation—or rather in the middle of a dispute. The contentious nature of the conversation provides an important lens for how we see the parable itself.

On first inspection, Luke's story may sound familiar to some readers. It should. A man approaches Jesus in public and asks, "What must I do to gain eternal life?" (10:25). Most readers regard the question as genuine, even though Luke tells us it is a hostile question that is meant to test Jesus. (More on that later.) We do so because we are familiar with very similar stories from Mark 10:17-22 (when a rich man asks the same question) and 12:28-34 (when a scribe inquires about the most important commandment). Luke has performed some very clever storytelling here, combining details from both stories—but especially adapting the story from Mark 12:28-34 in strategic ways. Let's take a closer look.

In Mark 10:17-22 a rich man asks Jesus what he must do to receive eternal life. We'll find basically the same story at Luke 18:18-23, where Luke modifies it only a little bit. The question is genuine in both accounts. Jesus replies by summarizing key commandments. The man rightly claims he has observed these commandments from his youth, but Jesus then requires him to divest himself of his possessions, give the proceeds to the poor, and follow Jesus. The man cannot bring himself to part with his wealth. Saddened, he leaves Jesus.

The story in Mark 12:28-34 occurs among a host of confrontations between Jesus and various authorities in Jerusalem, but this conversation stands out from the others. It is not confrontational. A scribe, probably Mark's equivalent of a legal expert, asks Jesus to identify the primary commandment. Jesus begins with the Shema, Judaism's great confession that God is one, and couples it with the command to love one's neighbor as oneself. The scribe agrees, and Jesus affirms his wisdom, sort of: "You aren't far from God's kingdom" (12:34). We should note here that Jesus answers the scribe's question in Mark, and Jesus affirms the scribe's wisdom.

Here's where things get dicey. Luke leaves out the story from Mark 12 but recycles it in a fascinating way to provide a context for the Samaritan parable. The sure sign that Luke has repurposed the story is that Luke 20 follows the sequence of stories that surrounds Mark 12:28-34—except that Luke omits that one passage with the scribe. Then Luke carefully adapts the story from Mark in the following ways:

- Luke keeps the scribe, turning him into a "legal expert," probably a different term for roughly the same role.
- Luke advances the story far ahead in the narrative, moving it out of Jerusalem early into Jesus' journey toward the Holy City. (If Luke followed Mark's sequence, it would belong between Luke 20:40 and 20:41.)
- Luke changes the conversation from a friendly one into a test.
- Luke changes the question from one about the primary commandment to one about receiving eternal life, the same question that will come up again in 18:18.
- And of course, Luke inserts the Parable of the Good Samaritan into the middle of the conflict.

Luke frequently places parables in contexts that provide explanations for the parable. We'll see this with the Parable of the Prodigal Son as well. In this case, the legal expert's question sets up Jesus' story, and Jesus' story turns the tables back on his questioner.

How Luke "Repurposes" Stories

Luke's repurposing of Mark's story of the scribe fits a pattern we see elsewhere in Luke's Gospel. Luke does this kind of thing several times with other stories from Mark. Luke shares about half of the material in Mark's Gospel. When Luke does so, Luke generally follows Mark's story in order, item by item. But Luke occasionally plucks a single story out of its sequence only to rework it somewhere else. The Parable of the Good Samaritan is a perfect example of Luke taking Mark's writing, changing it a little bit, inserting a story of his own, and, in this case, making a new and stronger point.

Conflict

Luke's crafting of the story transforms the legal expert from an earnest seeker to a hypocritical enemy. Luke describes his question as a "test" (10:25), using the same Greek word Luke uses for the three challenges the devil poses Jesus in the wilderness (4:1-13, *peirazo*). In other words, there's nothing friendly about this conversation. It is a public contest from the outset. Once readers grasp the hostile tone of this conversation, it will affect how they view everything else about the passage.

Let's reflect for a minute: what does it mean when someone asks us a question when they already think they know the answer? It's adorable when children do it with riddles. My grandson asked me the other day why the chicken crossed the road, and it delighted us both that I didn't know the answer! Thank goodness they're still coming up with new chicken/road jokes. Otherwise, it's rarely a good thing when someone questions us in this way. Lawyers are trained never to ask a question of a hostile witness without knowing the answer in advance. I suppose police detectives use the same technique. Even in the classroom, I try to avoid asking students questions that have only one correct answer: it shuts down discussion like bad breath.

Not that I've taught with bad breath. That was just an example.

Luke shapes the conversation to emphasize the legal expert's bad faith. In *Mark's* two stories, Jesus answers the questions he is asked. To the man who inquires how to receive eternal life, Jesus recites key commandments (Mark 10:17-19). And to the legal expert who asks about the primary commandment, Jesus replies with the two most important commandments (12:29-31). But notice how *Luke's* Jesus replies to the legal expert's hostile question:

"What is written in the law? How do you interpret it?" (10:26).

Instead of answering the man's question, Jesus turns it right back upon him.

When reading this passage, we can imagine an ancient Mediterranean society in which public conversation could be a form of combat. There could be friendly conversations, of course. Most were. But public confrontations also presented the opportunity for verbal showdowns. Many of us experienced our closest analogy to this sort of hostility in the hallways of junior high, just before classes began. But in the ancient world, such confrontations were real and common. We see one clear example in Luke, when Jesus receives criticism for healing on the Sabbath. Calling his opponents hypocrites, he points out that they would rescue their livestock, yet they complain when he heals a human being. Luke concludes the story: "When he said these things, all his opponents were put to *shame*, but all those in the crowd rejoiced at all the extraordinary things he was doing" (13:17).

The key word here is *shame*, a public verdict of disgrace. We see this pattern especially when Jesus enters Jerusalem. Luke 20 presents one scene after another in which various groups seek to best Jesus in a public confrontation. Luke wraps up the series of confrontations by declaring Jesus' public victory: "No one *dared* to ask him anything else" (20:40).

The legal expert knows the answer to his own question: love God, and love your neighbor (10:27). This is the classic answer, the same answer Jesus provides in Mark 12. The conversation could end here, with the legal expert mildly humiliated, when Jesus congratulates him—ironically, of course—for knowing the answer to his own question.

The context of verbal combat proves especially important when the legal expert simply cannot let things go. Our translations read,

"But the legal expert wanted to prove that he was right, so he said to Jesus, 'And who is my neighbor?'"

This is where many of us lose track of the story. Forgetting that the legal expert is operating in bad faith, we align our privileged perspective with his.

Here is the problem in a nutshell: we ourselves want to justify our sense of guilt about whatever moral concerns we have. We imagine the lawyer wanting to justify his lack of charity toward other people. But the legal expert is trying to recover his sense of public honor by advancing the debate with Jesus to a second question. We are trying to justify ourselves morally, while the legal expert wants to justify himself publicly. Having lost one abstract theological debate, he wants to start another one. He wants to save face.

Jesus replies to this second question with a parable—and he follows the parable with another question. Jesus' second question completely reverses the question Jesus is supposed to answer.

Legal Expert: "And who is my neighbor?" (10:29)	Jesus: "What do you think? Which one of these three was a neighbor to the man who encountered thieves?" (10:36)

The lawyer asks, "to whom am I obliged to give help?" Jesus rejects that question, presumably for two reasons. First, the question, being hostile, reflects bad motives. And second, the question reflects just the sort of privilege Jesus is out to undermine. Jesus' question is different: "Which of these three, does it seem to you, *was* a neighbor to the victimized man?" (paraphrased).

Jesus rejects the premise that we might *choose* our neighbors, insisting instead that we *become* neighbors.

It's all a bit much for the legal expert. Challenged to identify the neighbor in the parable, he knows the answer once again. "The one who demonstrated mercy toward him."

Jesus closes the argument. "Go and do likewise."

Working a Different Parable

By adapting Mark's story about the legal expert who asks Jesus a question into moment of conflict, Luke creates the perfect setting for the Parable of the Good Samaritan. The parable does not stand by itself. Instead, it serves to undermine the legal expert's logic. He wants to know who deserves his help, who is his neighbor. The parable rejects that question, the charity question.

Nor does the parable tell us we should go out and help Samaritans, exactly. Let's ponder that idea for a moment. The charitable interpretation of the Good Samaritan parable focuses on whom "we," the hearers of the parable, should help. By that logic, the parable should read differently. Maybe it would read like this:

> A certain man was walking down the road from Jerusalem to Jericho. He came upon a priest, who had been beaten by robbers, left naked and half-dead on the side of the road. He felt compassion for the priest, tended to his wounds, and took him to receive care. Then he came upon a Levite and treated the Levite in the same way. Finally, he came upon a Samaritan—a Samaritan, can you believe it!—and he offered the same help to the Samaritan!

This reworked parable fits the logic we generally assign to the parable in Luke 10:25-37 far better than it does the parable we actually encounter there.

To put it indelicately, the parable Jesus tells places the reader-hearer in the position of the help-ee and identifies the neighbor and the help-er. Our charitable interpretation, like the Good Samaritan laws, gets things exactly the other way around, turning ourselves into the Samaritans and the helpers. The parable begins by inviting readers to imagine themselves alongside the victim at the roadside, half naked and in desperate need of help.

Can We Have It Both Ways?

To this point I've worked very hard to challenge the usual charitable interpretation of the Good Samaritan parable. The charitable interpretation encourages readers to feel secure in our places of privilege. It aligns readers with the legal expert who asks, "Who is my neighbor?" Jesus rejects that question and the privileged subject position that it assumes.

Instead, Jesus tells a parable. We see this rejection in Jesus' follow-up. After demonstrating the Samaritan's compassionate action, Jesus asks, "Which one of these three was a neighbor to the man who encountered thieves?" (10:36). Jesus' question flips the script provided by the legal expert: the lawyer wanted a neighbor in need of help, but in Jesus' parable world the neighbor is the one providing help. Thus, the legal expert must answer: "The one who demonstrated mercy toward him" (10:37).

But parables are flexible; they can perform more than one job at a time. Jesus' parable does indeed reject the legal scholar's question. But having rejected the "Who is my neighbor?" question and the privilege that goes with it, Jesus then comes full circle: "Go and do likewise."

Jesus commands the legal expert to *stop evaluating* potential neighbors and *become* a neighbor. And . . . cut. Luke closes the scene there, Jesus having the last word.

The charitable interpretation is dangerous because it encourages Jesus' followers to assume a position of superiority with respect to other people. Jesus will have none of that, nor will Luke's Gospel. But neither is Luke satisfied with simple attitude adjustments. Of course, Luke wants followers of Jesus to act with compassion and justice. It simply makes all the difference how we do so.

For two years I was a member of a church in Charlotte, North Carolina, that provided winter shelter for the homeless on Saturday nights and breakfast on Sunday morning. Again, it's rare for prosperous churches to provide social services on Sunday mornings. Churches are fine offering services during the week, but we generally save our space for ourselves on Sundays. But this church opened its space for the homeless on Sundays.

One Sunday the pastor got an idea. He didn't just invite the church's homeless guests to worship. That was a given. It was a communion Sunday, so he asked a couple of the guests if they would like to *serve* communion to the congregation. The idea was theologically radical, demonstrating to all of us that a right relationship to Jesus depends on a right relationship to the poor. (Matthew 25:31-46, the Parable of the Sheep and the Goats, is often invoked to make this point.) The idea also gets right to the point of the Good Samaritan parable, flipping the script of who helps whom.

We continued this tradition with the Lord's Supper over a period of time. Looking back over twenty years, I'm still a little uncomfortable with it. I'm worried that it put poor people under an awkward spotlight and used them as lessons for the rest of us. I trust my former pastor. I know he spoke with them earnestly beforehand and graciously sought their permission, and I know this practice was significant to many people.

We never talked about it in these terms, but that congregation in Charlotte rehearsed the Parable of the Good Samaritan in a meaningful way. We offered hospitality to our neighbors who needed a warm place to sleep and a hot meal, then we turned around and received hospitality from those same neighbors at the communion table. We experienced neighborliness in both senses.

Chapter 5

Losing, Finding, Partying

The Parable of the Prodigal Son

Jesus said, "A certain man had two sons. The younger son said to his father, 'Father, give me my share of the inheritance.' Then the father divided his estate between them. Soon afterward, the younger son gathered everything together and took a trip to a land far away. There, he wasted his wealth through extravagant living.

"When he had used up his resources, a severe food shortage arose in that country and he began to be in need. He hired himself out to one of the citizens of that country, who sent him into his fields to feed pigs. He longed to eat his fill from what the pigs ate, but no one gave him anything. When he came to his senses, he said, 'How many of my father's hired hands have more than enough food, but I'm starving to death! I will get up and go to my father, and say to him, "Father, I have sinned against heaven and against you. I no longer deserve to be called your son. Take me on as one of your hired hands."' So he got up and went to his father.

"While he was still a long way off, his father saw him and was moved with compassion. His father ran to him, hugged him, and kissed him. Then his son said, 'Father, I have sinned against heaven and against you. I no longer deserve to be called your son.' But the father said to his servants, 'Quickly, bring out the best robe and put it on him! Put a ring on his finger and sandals on his feet! Fetch the fattened calf and slaughter it. We must celebrate with feasting because this son of mine was dead and has come back to life! He was lost and is found!' And they began to celebrate.

"Now his older son was in the field. Coming in from the field, he approached the house and heard music and dancing. He called one of the servants and asked what was going on. The servant replied, 'Your brother has arrived, and your father has slaughtered the fattened calf because he received his son back safe and sound.' Then the older son was furious and didn't want to enter in, but his father came out and begged him. He answered his father, 'Look, I've served you all these years, and I never disobeyed your instruction. Yet you've never given me as much as a young goat so I could celebrate with my friends. But when this son of yours returned, after gobbling up your estate on prostitutes, you slaughtered the fattened calf for him.' Then his father said, 'Son, you are always with me, and everything I have is yours. But we had to celebrate and be glad because this brother of yours was dead and is alive. He was lost and is found.' "

Luke 15:11-32

What do you think are the best-known Bible passages? Among the nominees I would have included Psalm 23, the Lord's Prayer (Matthew 6:9-13), maybe John 3:16, and two of the parables under consideration in this study: the Good Samaritan and the Prodigal Son.

The internet age, however, has made it entirely impossible to identify which passages are most familiar and best loved. Every year various search engines and Bible content sites publish their lists of most popular searches, most of which consist of single verses. Entire passages are left out. But surely the Parable of the Prodigal Son has made a deep impression on the Christian imagination. Rembrandt's classic painting inspired an entire book by the theologian and spiritual writer Henri Nouwen, and contemporary artists continue the tradition.[1] If Protestants in the United States have a "national hymn," it begins:

> Amazing grace, how sweet the sound
> That saved a wretch like me

I once was lost but now am found
Was blind but now I see.

The prodigal's story provides the template for every Christian conversion. Hank Williams lived the tune and wrote it too: "I wandered so aimless, life filled with sin."[2] Some of us found Jesus in churches that expected us to share our personal testimonies, the stories of how Jesus redeemed us from our sinful pasts. That proved hard work for me. Having found Jesus just before my fifteenth birthday, I was jealous of friends more accomplished in sin than I had been.

The Parable of the Prodigal Son is the longest and the most complex of Jesus' parables. It features four characters with speaking parts, along with a supporting cast. Although the parable is usually named after him, and although readers generally identify with him, the prodigal or younger son may be the least complicated of the three major characters. In Luke's telling, the parable is the third in a set of three parables. There's a lot more to say about the Parable of the Prodigal than simply to rehearse the story of the young man who was lost.

Three Parables

We do not know who wrote Matthew, Mark, Luke, or John. Many pastors and scholars doubt even the popular legend that Luke was composed by "Luke the physician." We can say, however, that all four Gospels reflect a high degree of narrative artistry. Luke 15 provides one very fine case study.

Our chapter and verse numbers were added long after the books of the Bible were composed, but Luke 15 constitutes a well-crafted set piece. The chapter opens by introducing a note of conflict.

All the tax collectors and sinners were gathering around Jesus to listen to him. The Pharisees and legal experts were grumbling, saying, "This man welcomes sinners and eats with them" (15:1-2).

This opening invites our curiosity. First, why would tax collectors and sinners gather around Jesus? We'll reflect on this question in a little more depth later, but for now let's begin with the obvious. Luke is suggesting that these social outcasts tended to seek Jesus out, that they enjoyed his company. What's more, they desire to hear his teaching. We should wonder what it is about Jesus that draws sinners into his presence so that they want to hear what this supposedly righteous teacher has to say.

The second matter is that the people who are criticizing Jesus on precisely this point are publicly righteous people, the Pharisees and the legal experts. Jesus does two things. He welcomes sinners. Rather than scolding them or rejecting them, he simply hangs out with them. And he eats with them. As in all cultures, table company is the sign of true fellowship. Your true friends are the people with whom you eat, especially if you eat in one another's homes.

Pharisees in Luke

The Pharisees play the role of Jesus' primary antagonists in all four Gospels. Luke, however, provides a slightly softer portrayal of the Pharisees than the other Gospels do, especially in comparison with Matthew and Mark. In Luke, Pharisees have Jesus over to eat (7:36-50; 11:37-54; 14:1-24). These events always lead to conflict, but at least the Pharisees try. At one point the Pharisees even warn Jesus of a plot against his life (13:31-35).

Historians question how accurately the Gospels portray the Pharisees. We have little direct evidence concerning how other ancient people regarded them, but it appears the Pharisees were widely respected by their contemporaries as people who simply tried to lead lives of purity and righteousness. In contrast, the Gospels portray them as power-hungry, hypocritical, and greedy. The apostle Paul reminds us that he had been a Pharisee (Philippians 3:6), and that's something he's proud of.

Luke follows this brief opening controversy with a series of three parables: the lost sheep (15:3-7), the lost coin (15:8-10), and the lost son, or Prodigal (15:11-32). Although the Parable of the Prodigal Son is much longer and far more complicated, these three parables all hold some things in common. Something is lost, obviously. The one who has lost the thing cares deeply about it. The shepherd foolishly abandons ninety-nine sheep to search for one lost sheep. The woman searches diligently for one lost coin. And while the father does not leave his household to seek his lost son—after all, the son had chosen to leave—he throws a marvelous party upon the son's return.

So things are lost. Things are found. Rejoicing happens upon their return. But there's one other item these stories share that's easily over-looked: food.

It may seem I am overstating the point. Obviously, the father in the Parable of the Prodigal Son provides a banquet. But the other two parables simply involve calling friends over to celebrate. They do not mention food explicitly. Just the same, it is difficult to imagine "celebrating" in a Mediterranean culture without food being shared. I think this issue will prove important.

The Parable of the Prodigal Son is longer than the other two parables for multiple reasons. For one thing, the third item in a series almost always gets more attention. We saw that dynamic in the Parable of the Good Samaritan. Moreover, a lost son is a human being, and he has a story of his own. That adds multiple layers of drama and requires a fuller telling. But there's also the matter of the older brother, an "extra" element in the parable. I would suggest the older brother draws the parable full circle. The elder brother believes it is inappropriate to throw a party for the younger brother who, after all, had left the household willingly. Does his criticism repeat the position held by the Pharisees and legal experts at the beginning of Luke 15? When the parable closes, we readers are left to wonder what will become of this older brother.

Sinners in Luke

The three Synoptic Gospels—Matthew, Mark, and Luke—all describe Jesus' companionship with sinners and tax collectors. One scene appears in all three Gospels: Jesus calls the tax collector Levi to become his disciple then enjoys a meal at Levi's house with "many" tax collectors and sinners. Legal experts associated with the Pharisees complain that Jesus eats with sinners and tax collectors, and Jesus replies: "Healthy people don't need a doctor, but sick people do. I didn't come to call righteous people, but sinners" (Mark 2:17).

The details vary among the three accounts (Matthew 9:9-13; Mark 2:13-17; Luke 5:27-32). Matthew's Gospel identifies the tax collector as Matthew rather than Levi. Matthew and Luke include Pharisees among those who weigh the complaint against Jesus. And Luke adds a note about repentance: Jesus calls sinners to repentance. Basically, however, the three accounts tell the same story.

Matthew adds another story about Jesus and sinners. John the Baptist, now imprisoned, sends messengers to Jesus: "Are you the one who is to come, or should we look for another?" (11:3). After Jesus sends his reply to John, he addresses the crowds about the opposition he and John face. John practices asceticism, neither overeating nor indulging in alcoholic beverages, and they accuse John of having a demon. Jesus does just the opposite, attending banquets and drinking, and people say, "Look, a glutton and a drunk, a friend of tax collectors and sinners" (11:19). Once again, we encounter the criticism that Jesus cavorts with tax collectors and sinners. Luke shares this story too (7:24-35).

Luke's Gospel goes out of its way to amplify this theme. It shares the one story about Levi the tax collector with Mark and Matthew. With Matthew it shares the accusation that Jesus is a glutton and a drunk. But several other stories occur only in Luke that feature Jesus' special relationship with sinners.

Sinners and Tax Collectors

Modern Christians struggle with the concept of sinners in the Gospels. "Aren't we all sinners?" we reason. But the Gospels reflect the reality of Jesus' world: some people were viewed as especially righteous, some were notorious sinners, and most people weren't regarded as especially noteworthy in either respect. The apostle Paul wrote that "All have sinned and fall short of God's glory" (Romans 3:23), but even he was happy to list categories of sinners who could not inherit the kingdom of God (1 Corinthians 6:9-10). This reality may not fit *our* theologies, but it does describe how biblical authors saw the world. (Read Psalm 1.)

The Gospels link sinners with tax collectors. Rather, they set forth tax collectors as a particular class of sinners. Tax collectors were essentially revenue collectors for the Romans. Contracted to glean tolls and tariffs on produce and other transported goods, tax collectors may have been perceived as Roman collaborators, as a drain on the local economy, as corrupt—or possibly as all of the above. In Luke the crowd regards the tax collector Zacchaeus as a sinner. In turn Zacchaeus acknowledges the association of tax collectors with corruption: "If I have cheated anyone . . ." (19:7-8).

Immediately following the visit from John's messengers, Luke adds an encounter between Jesus and a sinful woman. A Pharisee named Simon invites Jesus to dinner, and a sinful woman comes to anoint Jesus with ointment. Instead, her tears soak Jesus' feet, which she wipes with her hair. Keeping his thoughts to himself, Simon takes offense that Jesus would allow such intimate contact from such a sinful woman, but Jesus calls attention to the woman's kindness and pronounces her forgiveness (7:36-50).

Note the beginning of a pattern. Several elements appear once again: Jesus meets a sinner in a meal setting, and he receives criticism from a Pharisee, as he did in 5:27-32. Jesus' response to the accusation that he is a glutton and a drunk, a friend of tax collectors and sinners (7:34), another reference to his dining habits, closely follows Luke's notice that the Pharisees and legal experts had rejected John's baptism (7:30). The pattern consists of these elements: Jesus, sinners, meals, and complaints from Pharisees.

Let's pay attention and notice something the pattern lacks. Jesus never criticizes the sinners' behavior. He never tells them to change their ways. And even though Luke often speaks of repentance and celebrates repentance—perhaps Luke even shows sinners repenting—Jesus never directly calls sinners to repent.[3] Not in Luke, anyway.

Luke 15 marks our next set of examples. Three parables involving things lost and found, all followed by celebrations. The first two parables conclude with Jesus remarking upon how great joy breaks out in heaven over just one sinner who repents. The third parable shows us a son, once lost, who comes home, and the great party that celebrates his return. Just before these three parables is the complaint from the Pharisees and legal experts concerning Jesus' table company.

Vacation Bible school alumni know the next and final example: the story of Zacchaeus (19:1-10). The short tax collector climbs a sycamore tree to watch Jesus process into Jericho. Spotting him, Jesus invites himself into Zacchaeus' home. The Pharisees do not appear in this story. Nor does a meal occur, not explicitly. But if Jesus is to stay in Zacchaeus' house, surely one or more meals will occur. "Everyone" who watches grumbles that Jesus is going to visit a sinner.

Beyond this pattern Luke adds another parable, the Parable of the

Pharisee and the Tax Collector (18:9-14). Both men go to pray in the Temple. The Pharisee thanks God for making him the righteous person that he is, while the tax collector pleads God's mercy: "God, show mercy to me, a sinner." He doesn't even repent exactly. But it is the tax collector who returns home "justified" more than (or "rather than") the Pharisee.

In Mark and in Matthew it is striking that Jesus, a righteous teacher, would enjoy the company of sinners, especially at the table. Psalm 1 warns the righteous to avoid the company of sinners, after all. Luke's Gospel develops this theme into a major point of emphasis. This factor provides a larger context for Luke 15 and for the Parable of the Prodigal Son in particular.

Focus: The Younger (Prodigal) Son

The parable tells us less about the younger son than we might assume. He receives at least as much attention as any character in the parable, but we know perhaps less about his motives and his behavior than about those of his father and his brother. As with all three characters, in some ways, we don't know how things turn out for him. As C. H. Dodd warned us so long ago, parables tease our minds into active thought. They don't necessarily resolve into neat conclusions.

Without explanation, the younger son directly asks for his share of the inheritance. I've heard many preachers explain his request in these terms: he wants his father dead. That interpretation has always left me a bit uneasy. Preaching is hard work, and it's tempting to go for the dramatic point. The story just doesn't go that far. On the other hand, there's nothing in the story to suggest the younger brother intends to stay in relationship with his family. He apparently thinks he can get by on his share of the inheritance and sets out for "a far country," as the King James Version so poetically renders it (15:13 KJV). One doesn't expect him to return home.

Jesus' parables prefer to provoke our curiosity rather than to satisfy it. They leave gaps unexplained. I'd like to know *why* this younger son wanted to set off on his own, wouldn't you? It can be a healthy discipline *not* to pursue that line of curiosity, to allow the parable to set its own terms and hold our curiosity at bay. Certainly we should not impose our assumptions upon the story and read it as if we know what's on this young man's mind. Parables call for curiosity and wonder. They are not ours to control.

But a disciplined curiosity can be a good thing. If we can hold our questions loosely, suggesting possibilities rather than committing ourselves to just one option, it might be helpful to brainstorm the range of options. Perhaps the younger son is simply foolish; being young and inexperienced, he has no idea what he's getting into, and his youthful desire for adventure outstrips his judgment. His behavior suggests that may be the case, as he clearly has no sustainability plan for making his share of the inheritance last. But should we close off the possibility that something is pushing the younger son to leave home, either something inside himself or something wrong in the family dynamics? Without committing ourselves to an explanation, it may be good to remember that we do not know why the young man leaves home.

We can imagine the hurt. Cultures vary greatly in how they deal with the transition from childhood to adulthood. I can't read this story without recalling the day I drove off to college with my car all loaded up and my mom standing in the driveway, crying. I'd see her in just a few weeks, of course. Once I had children, her granddaughters, and we'd moved far away, she'd do the same thing many times from that same driveway. And her great-grandson, whom she'd see twice a year? Same scene. How, then, do a father and a brother deal with a son who moves to a "far country" just for the sake of getting away?

We also note the obvious. The story does not mention a mother or any other family members. We do not know why. The reasons may be literary—a good parable benefits from simplicity. We might also consider that many, many women died quite young in the ancient world. Due largely to risks associated with pregnancy and childbirth, a woman's average life expectancy in Jesus' world was probably between 25 and 30 years. Many adult sons may have survived their mothers.

The pain goes beyond family grief. The parable does not explain the calculations by which the father divides the inheritance. An effective parable must be economical. Nevertheless, the father could deny his son's request. When the younger brother walks away with his share of the inheritance, he has diminished the family's resources by one-third. That's nothing to sneeze at.

Stories Jesus Told

We might assume the family is well to do, maybe even rich. The parable gives away that they employ both hired laborers and enslaved persons, suggesting a substantial operation. The father has a special calf ready for a celebration, a ring and a "best" robe for the occasion, and the ability to gather musicians and dancers. Most readers imagine a wealthy family, and with reason—but again, the parable does not go into detail. Any household would feel the effect when one-third of its resources walks out the door.

The younger son reaches a moment of desperation. Jesus goes so far as to place him among the pigs, a clear sign that this Jewish young man has slipped below the line of degradation. I once interviewed an Israeli archeologist at the site thought to be the village of Cana, and I asked him how committed were Galileans in Jesus' time to observing the law of Moses. His response was immediate. "No pig bones. You won't find pig bones near a Galilean village." Here endeth the lesson. The younger son has reached desperate straits.

Yet there's still more we don't know—and this we would very much like to know. Does he seek reconciliation with his father? Or does he simply seek mercy? In other words, does this younger brother truly repent, or is he in survival mode—and does the difference make a difference?

Before we explore the evidence, let's remember Luke's emphasis on sinners and their need for repentance. Luke has already informed us that Jesus has come to call sinners to repentance (5:32). Twice in this very chapter Jesus invites his hearers to imagine the joy in heaven over sinners who repent (15:7, 10)—with sinners present who can overhear the conversation.

Yet in Luke, Jesus never directly criticizes a sinner or tells them to change. He has all kinds of harsh words for righteous and powerful people but none for sinners. Perhaps this accounts for why sinners seek his company (15:1-2). Luke provides a clear example of a sinner who expresses her devotion to Jesus. The sinful woman weeps at Jesus' feet and wipes his feet with her hair: is this repentance (7:36-50)? Likewise, in the Parable of the Pharisee and the Toll Collector, we see a sinner pleading for mercy. But does he change his ways (18:9-14)? Upon meeting Jesus, the tax collector Zacchaeus declares that he gives half his possessions to the poor, and if he defrauds anyone, he repays

76

them four times as much. Is this a moment of repentance, or has Zacchaeus been behaving this way all along (19:8)? (Zacchaeus speaks in the present, and not the future, tense, suggesting that he is defending himself.) Before we identify the younger son as a model of repentance, we should take a very close look at the story.

First, the younger brother has really messed up. Anyone can see that; it's beyond denying. Once on his own, according to a literal rendering of the Greek, he has scattered his livelihood in an undisciplined way. Back in the day we would have said he "blew" it. We can read into that all we want. Most readers see the younger brother as a profligate playboy through the eyes of the late English soccer star George Best: "I spent a lot of money on booze, birds and fast cars. The rest I just squandered."[4] Certainly his older brother sees things this way: "when this son of yours returned, after gobbling up your estate on prostitutes . . ." (15:30).

That's supplying a lot more information than Jesus' story begins with. Perhaps the older brother's assessment is uncharitable. But it's certainly within the realm of possibility, given the earlier description of the son's behavior. Similar fictions in ancient Greek literature confirm this suspicion: the young man is playing into a stereotype. He has messed up on a grand scale.

But does desperation imply repentance? Or does the younger brother's desperation simply lead him to a pragmatic plan of action? Here we might peek ahead, and just a few verses, to another character who encounters a similarly narrow pass. About to be tossed on the street, the dishonest manager of Luke 16:1-13 also talks to himself and comes up with a plan. There's no question of repentance there.

Luke says nothing directly about the younger brother's repentance. He realizes that even his father's hired workers have it better than he does. (That's a compliment to his father, by the way.) He chooses to request standing among them rather than among the enslaved workers, which is a prudent course of action. Some readers might conclude the younger brother is simply making the best of things. He returns home and executes his plan.

Yet there's something to be said for the younger brother as a model of repentance. First, there's the literary context. Luke 15 has twice announced the joy in heaven over sinners who repent. Second, this younger brother does confess his sin: "Father, I have sinned against heaven and against you. I no longer deserve to be called your son" (15:18-19). We might debate what, exactly, are his sins: his attitude toward his father and his household, his behavior while he's been away, or both. But he does acknowledge his sins. Finally, we might reckon with the cruel reality of repentance. Few of us repent simply because we have done wrong. We typically come to repentance when our behavior has led to pain—primarily to ourselves, but also for people we care about. We should not think less of repentance because it springs from desperation. That's how it works.

We might add one more consideration to the younger brother's return home. Shame is a factor in every culture, but social scientists categorize ancient Mediterranean societies like the Galilee of Jesus' day as "honor/shame" societies. In other words, the values of honor and shame functioned as primary motivators in people's behaviors. You and I may not be able to understand why many people just a few generations ago would have fought to the death over a public insult, but they did. Indeed, there are pockets of our own society in which that is the case today. That's an honor/shame dynamic. We are adding little to the story to assume that the younger son's decision to return home involved coming to terms with severe public humiliation.

Once welcomed home by his father, the younger brother's part in the story is done. Jesus will talk about him, but he no longer speaks or acts. His job is to behave poorly, lose everything, repent, and return home to a grand celebration. His father and his brother have a lot more work to do.

Focus: The Forgiving Father

Some people think we should rename this one The Parable of the Forgiving Father. The son's decision to leave home is surprising, his request to receive his inheritance ahead of time even shocking. But his father's behavior creates the parable's real tension. I'm not sure that renaming the parable would make much of a difference; the father's behavior already stands at the center of the parable.

The most remarkable thing the father does may be the most easily overlooked: he grants the younger son's request. By no means is the father obligated to disburse his wealth ahead of time. The inheritance laws granted a double share to the oldest brother. With two sons, two-thirds of the estate would go to the older brother, one-third to the younger. Needless to say, one-third of an estate is a significant loss. Complicating the loss, let's remember that this is an agrarian society: almost surely the father must divide property, livestock, and the like. From the very top, this parable launches into unfamiliar territory: the father sacrifices his wealth, perhaps his security, and imposes hardship upon himself, his older son, and the entire enterprise in response to the younger son's ill-advised request. He doesn't have to do any of it.

Most interpreters devote their attention to the father's response when his son returns home. And naturally so, for it is dramatic. He spots his son from a distance—as if he has been scanning the horizon one long day after another. He runs to the son. Some have suggested that an ancient Mediterranean father would run only in a genuine emergency, for running is undignified. Others reply that the return of a lost son is surely sufficient cause for excitement. The father runs.

In preaching there's a tendency to sensationalize the Gospels where sensationalism isn't necessary. The goal is understandable. No preacher wants a drowsy congregation. Unfortunately, the sensationalism habit often expresses itself in contrasting Jesus' behavior or his teachings with an imaginary and negative depiction of ancient Judaism. In the case of the Prodigal Son, some of us have heard that son would not expect a warm welcome from his father because of what he had done or that ancient fathers did not show affection to their children. Simply, hogwash. We have ample evidence of love and affection from ancient fathers, including Jewish fathers. Is it not enough simply to note that the father sees, feels compassion, runs, and hugs?

Perhaps, however, the next steps need our attention, for they create controversy. Not only does the father restore his son to the household, he bestows *signs of honor* upon this son. The best robe, a ring, and sandals must come out. The festal calf, the one just in case of a special event. Perhaps we are not surprised by the party—"this son of mine was dead and has come back to life! He was lost and is found!" (15:24)—but the signs of honor are remarkable in any context. Whatever shame this younger son has brought on himself, the father rejects.

Here we encounter a baffling tension in Jesus' teaching. On the one hand, Jesus proclaims the principle of divine economic inequity:

"I say to you that everyone who has will be given more, but from those who have nothing, even what they have will be taken away" (19:26). This strange saying in the Parable of the Pounds suggests that some receive divine favor—and good for them. But this same Jesus proclaims what looks like a contradictory principle: "Those who are last will be first and those who are first will be last" (13:30).

So how does it work in Jesus' world? Do those who start off ahead multiply their advantages, or does God reverse the balance books against those who begin with privilege? The younger son begins with much, loses it all, and finds himself restored—perhaps to even greater honor than he started with.

The focus shifts from the rejoicing father. He fails to reach out to his older brother, who has been in the field. It seems safe to assume that, while the father is celebrating the older brother is out working. That is a sharp contrast, one left unstated by the parable. But the parable is not finished with the father. For when his older son refuses to enter the party, the father once again surprises us.

He *begs* the older son to come into the party. He reasons with him. He addresses his son tenderly, calling him "Child" (15:31; most translations read "Son"). He assures the older son that the entire estate remains his. But he also explains the necessity of welcoming a lost son: "We *had to* celebrate and be glad," he says (15:32), because that's what we do when one's brother, presumed dead, comes home alive.

The father may have failed his older son. We'll have to think about that. But he reaches out to that son with extreme tenderness. Both sons are loved.

Focus: The Uninvited Son

The structure of Luke 15 comes full circle. The chapter opens with sinners and tax collectors enjoying Jesus' company, while Pharisees and legal experts complain about Jesus' table company. A third parable concerning things lost, things found, and the parties that ensue has reached its own party. The chapter closes outside the party, where the older son is "furious" (15:28). It's as if the older son has taken the seat of the Pharisees and legal experts.

The elder brother has some things to say. As so often happens when we complain, none of his complaints reflects well on him. Preachers have been quick to pile on.

The older son begins by establishing his own superiority and faithfulness. This is never a good look, especially when we're angry. Indeed, the older son has remained faithful to his father. He has probably worked very hard. But, as we all do when we are angry, he does not speak the language of love: "Look, for so many years I have *slaved* for you and never disobeyed your instruction" (15:29, literal translation). The younger son has injured his father—yes, and his brother, too—by abandoning the family, but how deeply does the older son's description of the relationship cut? *Slavery.* We are not off to a good start.

The older son may be correct in complaining that he has received no great feast. We could argue back and forth about whether he deserves one. Most readers would follow his logic on this point. But Luke 15 follows a different logic: it reserves the big parties to celebrate the finding of things lost. We readers may sympathize with the brother. If we do, we step outside the logic Jesus is applying.

Then there is older son's description of his younger brother. Countless preachers have observed the hostility embedded in this language. First, the younger son is "this son of yours" rather than "my brother." As far as the older son is concerned, at least in this moment, this younger son has no name and bears no relationship to himself. Second, consider how the older son characterizes his brothers' behavior: "gobbling up your estate on prostitutes" (15:30). How exactly does he know this? The story hasn't shared how the younger son squandered his fortune, nor has the older brother been told directly. His accusation may be entirely correct, as we have noted, but it emerges from his resentful imagination rather than from the terms of the story.

The older son's complaints emerge from his anger, an anger that may be well-justified. But it doesn't place the older son in a flattering light.

Despite his lack of charity, I sympathize with the old brother on one key point. Certainly he is correct about one thing: the younger brother has just wasted one-third of the household's resources, yet he is welcomed with a party. All the more galling, though, the older son remains in the field while the party takes off. No one, it seems, has bothered to look for him—and that includes his father. So familiar is this parable to many of us that we overlook this crucial detail. The older son finds out about the party by *hearing* the music and dancing. He is reduced to asking a slave what is going on.

Not only has the older brother never received a party of his own. *This* party breaks out, and no one has bothered to tell him. He receives no invitation and no notice.

The parable does not dwell on this point. For that reason, maybe we shouldn't either. But I do. Whether Jesus or Luke designed the parable with this hook in mind, it's at this spot that I get hung up. Why neglect the older brother?

At this point the parable touches many readers in a very sensitive place. Lots of people know what it's like to be treated less favorably than their siblings, whether by one or both parents. I've observed it in people I care about. The wound runs so deep, even well-healed scar tissue still hurts. One kind of wound goes back to childhood. Still another manifests itself when one sibling becomes an adult caregiver for a parent or other loved one. Such love may prove rewarding, but it's hardly glamorous. More often, it includes daily hard work. And it is remarkable how often the parent who receives all this love takes for granted the adult child who has held things together and fawns over the siblings who make their visits and offer their kisses and hugs but do not bear the burden of daily, sometimes backbreaking chores. A peculiar bitterness accompanies cases like this.

I do not wish to over-psychoanalyze the older son. The story tells us he is furious, and it includes his complaints. There's literary genius in the fact that he learns of the party by overhearing it. That factor activates the many readers who identify with him. They know what it is to be taken for granted.

In any event, the parable closes with a party inside. Two figures remain outside, the father and his angry son. Whether they will find reconciliation remains unsaid.

Where We're Left

The Parable of the Prodigal Son, being the longest and most complicated of Jesus' parables, allows readers to "finish" the story at different points. Many readers feel satisfied upon the younger son's return. Having identified with his journey from being lost to receiving such a gracious welcome, they perceive a story about grace and salvation. Other readers, perhaps more doctrinally inclined, focus upon the father. Almost inevitably we associate the father with God, so often addressed as Father. The father's story shows boundless forgiveness and grace, extending even to his outreach toward the older son. But other readers read all the way through the older son's story.

If we follow through with the older son, we tend to follow one of two paths. Each follows its own logic. The first path judges the son harshly. His self-righteousness aligns him with the Pharisees and legal experts. In the Gospels they stand in for the people who benefit from public displays of righteousness. But the Pharisees themselves may not have been so bad; Paul was one, and historical sources suggest they were widely admired. Whatever their historical reputation, the Pharisees and legal experts function as Jesus' antagonists who will do most anything to protect their status. Just as Jesus' opponents cannot abide his companionship with sinners, the older brother is embittered by the lavish welcome his poor brother receives. His overblown complaints— *slaving! prostitutes!*—effectively seal his indictment.

The second path identifies with the older son. His complaints may go too far, but he has a legitimate beef. If his father is so loving, surely he might spare a thought and invite this faithful son to the party.

Luke is fond of crisis parables. If we stop reading with the younger son, the parable includes one true crisis, and it is resolved. The younger son's crisis resembles that of other characters in Luke: a precipitous fall from a place of relative prosperity and security. Other characters who encounter such crises come to varied ends. For example, the unfortunate victim on the road to Jericho is rescued by the Samaritan (10:25-37), and the dishonest manager concocts a plan that provides him with a safety net. But others, like the rich fool (12:15-21) and the rich man who ignores Lazarus (16:19-31), come to disaster. The younger son takes responsibility for his plight, makes the journey home, and finds salvation—hardly too strong a word—in his father's arms.

Beyond the crisis confronted by the younger son, the parable concludes with two other characters in crisis. At the end of the scene, the older son faces a crisis of his own. To this point he has relied upon a secure home and a secure role. His brother's return has thrown everything akimbo. The secure home is still there waiting for him, but now the rules have changed. His relationship with his father depends on whether he can acknowledge the return of his brother. It may even depend upon whether he can celebrate that return.

For his part, the father desperately wants both boys home. He needs reconciliation with his older son too. The Bible can be shameless in demonstrating the extent to which God reaches out in search of us wayward mortals, shameless to the point of stretching our theologies. If ever we needed an image of divine vulnerability, of divine longing for reconciliation, the father's plight at the end of this parable offers that picture. Like his older son, he, too, is standing outside the party. We do not know how things will turn out.

Chapter 6

A Reversal of Fortune

The Parable of the Rich Man and Lazarus

"There was a certain rich man who clothed himself in purple and fine linen, and who feasted luxuriously every day. At his gate lay a certain poor man named Lazarus who was covered with sores. Lazarus longed to eat the crumbs that fell from the rich man's table. Instead, dogs would come and lick his sores.

"The poor man died and was carried by angels to Abraham's side. The rich man also died and was buried. While being tormented in the place of the dead, he looked up and saw Abraham at a distance with Lazarus at his side. He shouted, 'Father Abraham, have mercy on me. Send Lazarus to dip the tip of his finger in water and cool my tongue, because I'm suffering in this flame.' But Abraham said, 'Child, remember that during your lifetime you received good things, whereas Lazarus received terrible things. Now Lazarus is being comforted and you are in great pain. Moreover, a great crevasse has been fixed between us and you. Those who wish to cross over from here to you cannot. Neither can anyone cross from there to us.'

"The rich man said, 'Then I beg you, Father, send Lazarus to my father's house. I have five brothers. He needs to warn them so that they don't come to this place of agony.' Abraham replied, 'They have Moses and the Prophets. They must listen to them.' The rich man said, 'No, Father Abraham! But if someone from the dead goes to them, they will change their hearts and lives.' Abraham said, 'If they don't listen to Moses and the Prophets, then neither will they be persuaded if someone rises from the dead.' "

Luke 16:19-31

In the "Parable Popularity Contest," the Parable of the Rich Man and Lazarus lags well behind the Samaritan and the Prodigal Son—but it is quite well known in its own right. The Samaritan and the Prodigal are much loved. We have suggested their popularity may result from being misunderstood and sentimentalized. But the Parable of the Rich Man and Lazarus troubles all kinds of interpreters. Popular versions of the first two parables conform to our cherished beliefs, but this parable of a rich person, a poor person, and their very different fates resists our familiar theologies and provokes us to seek alternative explanations. A rich man descends to Hades, while a poor man resides in Abraham's bosom—apparently a straightforward reversal of their earthly lives. That story line fits none of our cherished theological assumptions, and it makes many of us quite uncomfortable.

Our discomfort arises from what happens to the Rich Man, known in Christian tradition as Dives, which means simply "Rich Man" in Latin and archaic English. One could easily understand the parable as assuming a final judgment based upon "good works." The Rich Man endures torment, apparently because he neglected poor Lazarus. But we Protestants celebrate the doctrine of salvation by grace through faith. That means we reject the notion that our salvation depends upon anything we do or fail to do. We cannot "earn" our salvation through good works, we believe. Yet the parable clearly places the Rich Man in torment while Lazarus reclines in Abraham's bosom, and without much explanation.

Early commentators on the passage condemn the Rich Man for ignoring Lazarus. It is easy to reach that conclusion: the poor man is lying right outside the gate, and the Rich Man does nothing for him. The parable itself does not say that the Rich Man *ignored* Lazarus, only that he was feasting while Lazarus was suffering. From Lazarus' perspective, it makes no difference whether the Rich Man has noticed him or not: he remains miserable and hungry in either case.

Our second point of discomfort relates to ourselves. As with the Parable of the Good Samaritan, we do not want the sharp end of the parable pointing at us. We may have theological problems with eternal punishment as the outcome of simply doing nothing, but we also don't want ourselves examined according to Jesus' exacting standards. A vast gap separates our world from that of Jesus. In our world, we are keenly aware of poverty but we live in a different zip code. Most of us have some discretionary income, so our struggle involves the sense that perhaps we aren't doing enough to help. In Jesus' world, the vast majority of people struggled to survive from season to season, a few people enjoyed a measure of security, and only a tiny elite could be considered wealthy. As a result, many modern readers can identify with the Rich Man more easily than we can with Lazarus. That's an uncomfortable place from which to read this parable.

Literary Context

The literary context of the parable—or the surrounding verses and chapters in the Gospel—offers a number of clues for interpreting its meaning. The parable begins with the words, "A certain rich man" (16:19). Luke sometimes places parables in contexts that guide our interpretation. The Parable of the Good Samaritan pops up in the middle of the "Who is my neighbor?" conversation, while the Prodigal appears in the sequence of things-lost-and-found parables introduced by the complaint concerning Jesus' table company. At other points, Luke tells us how we should interpret a parable. The Parable of the Widow and the Dishonest Judge is introduced as a parable about persistence in prayer (18:1), and the Parable of the Pharisee and the Tax Collector specifically targets "people who had convinced themselves that they were righteous and who looked on everyone else with disgust" (18:9). The Parable of the Rich Man and Lazarus arrives without such packaging.

The parable does not lack for context, though. Chapter 15 of Luke closes with the Parable of the Prodigal Son, then Jesus turns his attention to teaching his disciples (16:1). Chapter 16 of Luke begins with the Parable of the Dishonest Manager (16:1-13). Like the

Parable of the Rich Man and Lazarus, the Dishonest Manager begins with the phrase, "A certain rich man." The man receives an accusation that the manager is squandering the rich man's property. Anticipating being fired and desperate to secure a home for himself, the manager bargains down the loans the rich man has extended to various debtors. In the end, the rich man (or "the Lord" in Greek) praises the corrupt manager for his sagacity. Lots of people struggle to explain why Jesus would tell a parable in which the hero is such a scoundrel. Commentaries on the passage often begin with words like, "This is the most challenging of Jesus' parables." We won't try to resolve that problem, but we can note that the parable concludes with a series of sayings attributed to Jesus, all perhaps partial explanations of the parable. Jesus' words conclude: "You cannot serve God and wealth" (16:13). The topic of wealth and how to relate to it is now on the table.

Luke and Wealth

Interpreters note that Luke stands out among the Gospels for its interest in wealth and possessions. Before giving birth to Jesus, Mary praises the God who "has filled the hungry with good things and sent the rich away empty-handed" (1:53). Shepherds, not magi with expensive gifts, receive the announcement of the Savior's birth and travel to honor the child (2:8-20). The first example of Jesus' teaching that Luke provides includes a reading from Isaiah that proclaims "good news to the poor" and liberation for the oppressed (4:18). In contrast with Matthew's Beatitudes, where Jesus blesses the "hopeless" (5:3), Luke's Jesus blesses the poor and pronounces woe upon the rich (6:20, 24). The issues of status and possessions pop up throughout the Gospel, not least in Luke's parables. The Parable of the Rich Man and Lazarus may be the most obvious example, but it does not stand alone. When Luke's Gospel closes and Luke's story moves on to the book of Acts, we find the early believers sharing their possessions with one another as needs emerged (Acts 2:44-45; 4:34-35).

Yet as much as Luke features wealth, poverty, and possessions, the Gospel's bottom-line teaching on these subjects remains unclear. Some passages, like Mary's song and Jesus' hometown sermon, sound revolutionary. Others seem more inclined toward charity rather than a restructuring of society. Some interpreters regard Luke as "the Gos-

> pel for the poor." More see Luke addressing believers who enjoy status and means with a warning. Their security is only temporary. It may well depend on how they relate to the poor.

Perhaps Jesus has turned toward his disciples, but make no mistake: the Pharisees remain nearby (16:14). We've encountered the Pharisees several times in Luke's Gospel. But now we get additional information: they are "money-lovers." As we turn toward the Parable of the Rich Man and Lazarus, our ears are attuned to the topic of wealth and the wealthy.

Sure enough, ours is the third parable in Luke that begins, "A certain rich man." The Parable of the Rich Fool starts off the same way (12:16). So does the parable that immediately precedes the Parable of the Rich Man and Lazarus (16:1). The "certain rich man" plays a minor role in the Parable of the Dishonest Manager, which directs its spotlight toward the scoundrelly manager. But the Parable of the Rich Fool is all about, well, the rich fool. Like the Rich Man who takes no effective notice of Lazarus, the Rich Fool also finds himself surprised by death. The Parable of the Rich Man and Lazarus contributes to a much broader theme in Luke's Gospel, where poverty, possessions, and people's relationships with them are a primary concern.

The parable's literary context includes one other significant detail. Jesus condemns the Pharisees for justifying themselves before other people yet deeply offending God (16:15). We encountered this language of justification in the legal expert who challenges Jesus: he wants to avoid embarrassment by asking Jesus another question (10:29). The CEB reads that the legal expert "wanted to prove that he was right," but this translation obscures that Luke is using the same verb translated "justify" in 16:15. The verb will appear again in the Parable of the Pharisee and the Tax Collector, involving who is justified in the sight of God (18:14).

We should also attend to what Jesus says to the Pharisees in this passage, since it comes immediately before the Parable of the Rich Man and Lazarus. Condemning the Pharisees' behavior, Jesus says, "Until John, there was only the *Law and the Prophets*" (16:16, emphasis added). In our parable, the Rich Man will ask that Lazarus warn his brothers, lest they share his fate. Abraham rejects the request:

"They have *Moses and the Prophets*. They must listen to them" (16:29, emphasis added).

The Law and the Prophets set the standard by which Jesus judges human behavior.

Another Character, Another Crisis

The Rich Man and Lazarus is the third Lukan parable we've encountered in this study. All three occur only in Luke. All three also belong to the category of crisis parables, in which a character begins in a relatively secure state, only to find that security taken away.

Some crisis parables present the opportunity for a happy ending. The Good Samaritan (10:25-37) and the Prodigal (15:11-32) do. The victim attacked by robbers receives the care he needs, although he's done nothing on his own part to address his emergency. How could he? The Prodigal returns home to his father's exuberant welcome. Although the parable closes with his father and brother standing outside the party, opportunity for reconciliation is there. The most entertaining of the crisis parables features the Dishonest Manager (16:1-13). Having lost his position, he crafts a lovely scheme: at the expense of his master, but to the benefit of the debtors, he earns hospitality in the debtors' homes.

In Luke's two "Rich Man" parables, the Rich Fool and the Rich Man and Lazarus, the rich man confronts a crisis he cannot avoid: death. (The Parable of the Dishonest Manager also begins with a "rich man," but he is not the central character and does not arrive at a crisis.) While death may provide a happy ending for Lazarus, that is far from the case with the two rich men. When the first rich man dies, God declares him a fool because he is not rich toward God. The second rich man, the one in our parable, finds himself tormented in Hades. Neither rich man enjoys an opportunity to resolve his crisis in a happy way. Death sees to that.

Several of Luke's parables provide "inside views" of their characters. We call this technique "interior monologue," where we readers "overhear" the character's personal thoughts. This happens only in Luke, and it reflects Luke's talent and artistry as a writer. The Rich Fool expresses his thoughts during this life. His thoughts portray his arrogance and short-sightedness. He makes quite the speech:

A Reversal of Fortune

What will I do? I have no place to store my harvest! Then he
thought, Here's what I'll do. I'll tear down my barns and build
bigger ones. That's where I'll store all my grain and goods. I'll
say to myself, You have stored up plenty of goods, enough for
several years. Take it easy! Eat, drink, and enjoy yourself.

Luke 12:17-19

Luke is showing off his education here. The Rich Fool's speech
echoes sentiments popular among ancient philosophers. The Epicure-
ans, for example, taught that we should live so as to maximize pleasure
and minimize pain. This life is all we have, after all, so we should
make the most of it. They did not mean that people should spend all
their time eating, drinking, and partying: too much of a good thing
leads to more pain than pleasure. But they did believe in making life
as pleasant as possible. The Rich Fool's speech also echoes another
philosopher to a striking degree, the Teacher of Ecclesiastes:

So I commend enjoyment because there's nothing better for
people to do under the sun but to eat, drink, and be glad.
This is what will accompany them in their hard work, during
the lifetime that God gives under the sun.

Ecclesiastes 8:15

It's easy to see that Luke's Jesus rejects these philosophies—the
Rich Man's monologue sounds ironic on a first hearing.

In the Parable of the Rich Man and Lazarus, however, we hear no
internal monologue. The Rich Man speaks only on the other side of
death, and he speaks to Father Abraham. Like the Prodigal and the
Dishonest Manager, he recognizes the depth of his plight, but he also
knows death's profound implications. Rather than ask for outright
salvation, he requests simply a little water to cool his tongue. Denied
even that comfort, he requests help for his brothers—someone needs
to warn them what lies beyond the grave.

One factor shows the truth behind the Rich Man's goodwill. With
each request, he asks Abraham to send Lazarus on his behalf: Lazarus
to cool his tongue with a drop of water, and Lazarus to warn his
brothers. *Now we know the truth:* the Rich Man *has* noticed Lazarus.
He recognizes Lazarus beyond the grave, so he must have observed
Lazarus lying at his gate. The Rich Man is guilty.

Not only is he guilty, the Rich Man still regards Lazarus as his inferior. Otherwise, why ask Abraham to treat Lazarus like a servant, fetching water and delivering messages? We may not hear the Rich Man's internal thought processes directly, but his speech gives them away. He *always* saw Lazarus, yet he did not help. He *still* sees Lazarus, yet he imagines himself as Lazarus' superior. But things have changed.

Theologies in the Way

Modern readers commonly raise two theological concerns about this parable: (1) does it contradict the doctrine of justification by grace through faith, and (2) does it present a full-blown account of judgment?

I don't know the answer to either question, but we are able to consider some evidence that may help us sort through it. Before we go there, we should prepare for the possibility that the parable might still leave us uncomfortable.

Christians, and especially Protestants, treasure the doctrine of justification by grace. Knowing our own imperfections, we confess that all of us live under sin. While we may grow in moral character in our lifetimes, none of us ever fully arrives. Moreover, we find it impossible to live free from sin, whether our own individual failings, the effects of others' behavior upon us, or our entrapment in harmful social systems that transcend our capacity to make individual choices. The only way out, we believe, is for God to save us. We cannot do it for ourselves.

In an important way we derive this doctrine from Paul. It appears especially in a few of his letters, specifically the ones that address the relationship between Jewish and Gentile believers in the church: Galatians, Romans, and Ephesians. In a larger sense, Paul did not invent this idea. Ancient Israel also knew human imperfection and believed that our only hope lies with God. When Moses receives a vision of God, but only from behind, the Lord proclaims God's own mercy and capacity to forgive (Exodus 34:6-7). Psalm 86 returns to the same language, voicing confidence in God's mercy and forgiveness. The God of the Old Testament is not different from the God of the New Testament. Both testaments witness to the same one God, who is merciful and gracious.

The Gospels all participate in this knowledge of God's grace. Jesus pronounces forgiveness freely (Luke 5:20; 7:48; 23:43). But the Gospels also care about human behavior, as does Paul (Romans 2:5-11; Galatians 6:7-8; see Revelation 20:12).

The Rich Man has neglected Lazarus. In the parable, this is the basis for his judgment. Abraham's first response to the Rich Man is vague on this point: "Child, remember that during your lifetime you received good things, whereas Lazarus received terrible things. Now Lazarus is being comforted and you are in great pain" (16:25).

From this response Abraham suggests only that the Rich Man and Lazarus have switched places. Lazarus now resides in blessed comfort, the opposite of his mortal state, and the Rich Man suffers the other side of this reversal. But we remember: the Rich Man's request reveals that he *saw* Lazarus and *did nothing*. Moreover, he wants to *warn* his brothers, a desire that also shows that he understands the logic of his judgment. Just in case we're slow to catch on, Abraham drives the point home: they have Moses and the prophets. They know the rules.

Some of us would turn to Paul for refuge: "Save us, Paul, from a fate that corresponds to our lack of compassion!" But our Apostle can sound very much like Father Abraham:

> On the one hand, he will give eternal life to those who look for glory, honor, and immortality based on their patient good work. But on the other hand, there will be wrath and anger for those who obey wickedness instead of the truth because they are acting out of selfishness and disobedience.
>
> Romans 2:7-8

Some readers of Paul might argue that this quotation is taken out of context, that Paul is really preparing the ground for his argument that God does *not* in fact judge according to our works. It's a complicated question. Let us simply consider the possibility that it matters what we do in this life—specifically, how we relate to the poor—and it matters more than we might be willing to appreciate.

The second question involves our notions of the afterlife. In the parable, Lazarus and the Rich Man arrive at their separate fates immediately upon death. We note that the Rich Man receives a burial, but that may not be so for Lazarus. Ancient readers cared very much about proper burial and would not have overlooked this detail. Luke says little about what happens right after we die, but one other passage is highly suggestive. Only Luke includes the conversation Jesus holds with his fellow crucifixion victims. One mocks Jesus. The other, defending Jesus, implores, "Jesus, remember me when you come into your kingdom" (23:42).

Perhaps we all know Jesus' response: "I assure you that today you will be with me in paradise" (Luke 23:43). Once again, we meet the notion that upon death mortals go immediately to their postmortem destination.

Luke uses some terminology that may give us pause. The Rich Man goes to *Hades*, which is a place of torment. The angels carry Lazarus to *Abraham's bosom*. And Jesus promises *paradise* to his crucified neighbor. None of these terms corresponds precisely to our common notions of heaven and hell. Hades is taken from Greek cosmology, a realm of the dead that could include places of punishment *and* places of blessing. The precise meaning of Abraham's bosom is less clear. Paradise is likewise unknown. One ancient Jewish text may provide some help. The *Testament of Abraham* depicts Abraham in paradise. There the righteous dwell, with Isaac and Jacob residing in Abraham's bosom. In that place there is no labor, no grief, and no mourning but peace and exaltation and eternal life (20:14).

Most interpreters understand Luke to promote a view of the afterlife in which one of two things occurs. One option is that people go to a temporary dwelling place until the final judgment. In this view Hades and paradise represent the two options for this in-between state. Few contemporary Christians hold this view, but some ancient Jews and Christians did. The other option is that Luke believes we arrive at our final destinations immediately after death.

The Afterlife in Ancient Judaism and Christianity

Luke, like Mark and Matthew, relates a debate between Jesus and the Sadducees concerning the Resurrection (20:27-40). The Sadducees, who do not believe in the Resurrection, challenge Jesus with a trick question. Imagine a woman who marries seven brothers according to the custom of levirate marriage. In the Resurrection, who is her husband? The background to this debate, of course, is that Sadducees do not believe in the Resurrection. Pharisees do, but Sadducees don't.

But why not? Simply, resurrection was a fairly new idea in Jesus' day. Apart from the book of Daniel, the Hebrew Scriptures do not include a clear doctrine of the afterlife. The primary view is that upon death we go to Sheol, a murky place where even the worship of God may be absent (Psalm 88:6-11). The concept of resurrection emerged in the centuries just before Jesus' time, and people apparently held quite diverse ideas about it. For example, consider Revelation 20:13, which depicts the sea giving back its dead. Many interpreters believe this passage is meant to counter the fear that people who do not receive proper burial can participate in the Resurrection.

We should probably be careful about drawing specific conclusions about the afterlife from this parable. To begin with, it's a parable. Jesus' parables are fictions meant to spur reflection on critical questions; they are not doctrinal essays. Moreover, the New Testament itself provides diverse views of the afterlife. Paul believed that dead people are just that—dead—until the final resurrection. At least early in his career he did not believe people move on to the afterlife immediately upon death (1 Thessalonians 4:16; 1 Corinthians 15:20-23). Paul may have changed his mind to the view that believers dwell with Christ immediately after death (Philippians 1:23).

We don't have to be too distressed by this ambiguity. People hold all kinds of beliefs about the afterlife. A close look at our churches' funeral liturgies shows that they avoid being overly specific about how things work out. Surely it is enough to believe that through Jesus' resurrection we all receive the hope of eternal life in God's presence.

The Parable of the Rich Man and Lazarus does raise questions of justification and the afterlife, but it remains a parable. We should take caution not to push the parable too far on either issue. We should be even *more* cautious, however, not to dismiss it. There's a sweet spot somewhere between turning a parable into a doctrinal statement and ignoring the issues it addresses. I recommend taking the parable seriously—and holding our judgments lightly. Luke is serious about the afterlife. Pointedly, Luke links our afterlife hope with how we relate to the poor.

Reversal or Warning?

Interpreters often characterize Luke's Gospel in terms of "The Great Reversal," the idea being that Luke's story flips the script on several social hierarchies, such as wealth and status, gender, righteousness, and even cultural-religious privilege.

In a world where the rich dominate the poor, Luke has angels proclaim the "good tidings" of Jesus' birth to shepherds rather than rulers. Jesus describes his message as good news for the poor and for prisoners, a message with particular resonance for readers whose nation incarcerates more of its citizens than any other. Three parables begin with "a certain rich man," all of whom meet difficulty.

Luke was written in a highly patriarchal society, yet Luke's Gospel features more stories involving women than any other. Luke's heroines include faithful Elizabeth and her fierce relative Mary, the women who can afford to support Jesus and his disciples out of their possessions (8:1-3), the sister disciples Martha and Mary who follow Jesus in different ways (10:38-42), the Persistent Widow who prevails in her pursuit of justice (18:1-8), and the women who testify first to the empty tomb—only to be disregarded by their male colleagues (24:1-12).

Luke emphasizes Jesus' ministry to sinners far more intensely than do the other Gospels. In Luke we see the party with Levi the tax collector (5:27-32), the encounter with the sinful woman (7:36-50), the parables of things lost and found (15:1-32), the Parable of the Pharisee and the Tax Collector (18:9-14), and the intrepid Zacchaeus who climbs the tree for a glimpse of Jesus (19:1-10). Heaven rejoices more over the repentance of one sinner than over the ordinary behavior of those who seem righteous.

And Luke shows more interest in God's blessing to Samaritans and to Gentiles than do the other Gospels. Samaritans figure three times in Luke's account (9:52-56; 10:25-37; 17:11-19) but zero in Matthew and Mark. Well, there is an exception: Matthew's Jesus instructs his disciples *not* to visit Samaritans (10:5). John, of course, includes the famous story of Jesus' encounter with a Samaritan woman (4:1-42). But Luke introduces Jesus' relevance for Gentiles even in his infancy (2:32), and Jesus will inaugurate his public ministry by pointing out how Elijah and Elisha healed Gentiles rather than Israelites (4:16-30).

Interpreters universally agree upon Luke's interest in the poor, in women, in sinners, and in Gentiles. But because we'd lose our jobs if we agreed on everything, we debate how thoroughly the idea of reversal applies to some of these categories. Does Luke really call for the poor to displace the rich, or is Luke satisfied with charity? Does Luke extend full equality to women, or does Luke include women only within a traditional range of roles?

Reversal certainly applies to the Rich Man and Lazarus. When the Rich Man approaches Abraham, the reply he receives is striking. "Child, remember that during your lifetime you received good things, whereas Lazarus received terrible things. Now Lazarus is being comforted and you are in great pain" (16:25).

If that's not reversal, what could possibly qualify?

But Abraham's reply also raises a question. Are we to take the parable as an official rule regarding humans and the afterlife, or should we construe it as Luke's way of warning those who are too comfortable in their privilege? Luke's story features people of means who demonstrate their righteousness, folks like the women who patronize Jesus' ministry (8:1-3) and Joseph of Arimathea, who sees to Jesus' burial (23:50-56). As Luke's story continues in Acts, believers use their wealth to look after one another (2:44-45; 4:34-35), and prosperous believers provide charity and support the early missionaries (9:36-39; 16:11-15). It seems that Luke's Jesus has room for persons who use their wealth to good ends. The Rich Man who ignores Lazarus does not stand in that company.

Self-Interested Indifference

Many worship services include a public confession of sins. The first service of word and table in the *United Methodist Book of Worship* includes this confession:

> Merciful God,
> we confess that we have not loved you with our whole heart.
> We have failed to be an obedient church.
> We have not done your will,
> we have broken your law,
>   we have rebelled against your love,
>   we have not loved our neighbors,

and we have not heard the cry of the needy.
Forgive us, we pray.
Free us for joyful obedience,
    through Jesus Christ our Lord. Amen.[1]

With this prayer we confess both sins of omission and sins of commission; that is, we confess what we have failed to do and the bad things we have actually done. Most confessions do so, often with the classic phrase, "by what we have done and by what we have left undone." As we confess it in worship, sin involves both categories.

In my experience, however, our imaginations weigh sins of *commission* far more heavily than those of *omission*. We tend to identify sin with misbehavior. Let's face it: we give more attention to some sins than to others. Sexual sins seem to top the list, although we don't all agree on what sexual behaviors count as sinful, with sins like lying and cheating coming in close behind. It's easier to point out a sin like adultery—some people did this and that, and other people were hurt—than to pinpoint sinful patterns and attitudes. Bitterness, enmity, greed, and gossip all are corrosive, but we generally don't call them "sins."

For a great moral teacher, Jesus does not seem particularly concerned with the sins that preoccupy us today. This is especially so in Luke, where he gains notoriety for hanging around with sinners—in a world quick to identify some as sinners and others as righteous. He does call out the "den of robbers" who run the Temple (19:46). On the whole, Jesus spends his energy on healing and teaching rather than on condemning personal moral failures.

According to Luke, one category of sin does hold Jesus' attention: self-centered indifference, or knowing about the needs of others and not caring. Jesus never names this sin, but it manifests itself throughout the Gospel. The Parable of the Rich Man and Lazarus constitutes Exhibit A of this pattern. Lazarus lies destitute, hungry and in pain, while the Rich Man goes on with his feasting. As the parable develops, we learn that the Rich Man knew about Lazarus all along, for he recognizes his poor neighbor in the afterlife. He even desires that Lazarus run his errands! The Rich Man sins not in being rich but in neglecting the need of his neighbor.

Luke's Gospel surrounds the Rich Man with good company.

There's the Rich Fool who focuses on his own security and happiness, storing treasure for this life but neglecting to accumulate treasure in heaven (12:15-21). Neither story shows outright oppression of the poor; rather, the rich men err in tending only to their own business. The Dishonest Judge does not set out to oppress the Widow; he'd much rather avoid her (18:1-8). When people are more concerned with their own affairs than with the things of God and the needs of others, they fail to follow Jesus (9:57-62; 14:15-24). Self-centered indifference poses a grave spiritual danger. It poses as taking care of one's own business, but it prevents people from tending to things more essential (21:34). This may account for Jesus' saying it is "very hard" for the rich to enter God's kingdom (18:24-25).

Parables rarely deliver doctrinal messages. Perhaps none of Jesus' parables addresses our speculative doctrinal questions. This is not to deny their theological value, for parables open us to a world in which God acts graciously and fearsomely. They reveal God's generosity as well as God's justice. Perhaps the Parable of the Rich Man and Lazarus conveys a doctrine of the afterlife. More likely, the parable invites us to read ourselves into its world and to reflect on that experience.

When we enter the world of the Rich Man and Lazarus, our options are narrow. We may identify ourselves with Lazarus. Certainly we all find ourselves in need of help from time to time. But if you are reading this study, chances are your life aligns far more readily with that of the Rich Man. Mine does. No, I'm not rich. Yes, I'm very much busy with my marriage, our children, my work, and my community involvement. But I also possess the capacity to live differently. So will most readers. The need that surrounds us is overwhelming, more than our imaginations can process. But what about the need right at our doors?

We have Moses and the Prophets. Will we listen to them?

Afterword

This study invites us to consider the parables and the assumptions we bring to them. Jesus' most distinctive teaching comes through the parables. Jesus didn't invent the form. We encounter parables in the Jewish Scriptures and rabbinic writings. The Greek and Latin rhetoricians discussed how to compose and use a parable. But Jesus' parables are distinctive: more than other ancient parables we know about, they challenge readers and hearers to think for themselves. As John Dominic Crossan observed, "When Jesus wanted to say something very important about God he went into parable."[1]

Only by devoting a significant period of time to the parables can we learn how to interpret them. I'm not saying there is just one way to read a parable. I am saying we can't learn to read and appreciate the parables without spending some focused time with them.

It's one thing to encounter an individual parable in a worship service, study group, or personal devotions. When we hear the parables in isolation from one another, as we generally do, we lack the opportunity to pause and reflect on what the parables have in common (and what they don't) or to consider how parables work. Experienced by itself, a parable will yield to just about any ingenious interpretation—from conventional ones that have held up for centuries to fairly nutty ones. No, the Parable of the Good Samaritan (Luke 10:25-37) is not an allegory about how we fall into sin, only for Jesus to bind our wounds and save us. That interpretation was very popular in the medieval period, and it isn't particularly harmful, but that's not what the parable is doing. No, Jesus did not promote capitalism in the Parable of the Talents/Pounds (Matthew 25:14-30; Luke 19:11-27). Bankers and interest-based lending did exist in Jesus' time, but the theory of capitalism did not. The parable is not a case study in modern economics.

But it's another thing to consider the parables together. This study surveys several very different parables. The Parable of the Sower (Mark 4:1-20) presents itself as an allegory in which every kind of soil invites us to consider the many kinds of responses to Jesus' ministry. Every parable has elements that map onto realities beyond the world of the parable, but not every parable is an allegory. We discover that not all parables are alike.

What other lessons come through? First, whenever we interpret ancient literature, including the Bible, it's essential to take account of the ancient historical and cultural context. This lesson is scarcely unique to the parables, but it is essential. Sometimes we have the information we need: we know about enmity between ancient Judeans and Samaritans, for example, and we understand how Jewish inheritance customs bear upon the Parable of the Prodigal Son (Luke 15:11-32). But sometimes we lack information we'd desperately like to have. Did ancient farmers scatter seed randomly, striking promising and unpromising soil alike? We wrestled with that question when we read the Parable of the Sower. Did a denarion represent a standard day's wage, as we tend to assume? This question seems important for the Parable of the Workers in the Vineyard (Matthew 20:1-16), and we wish we knew how many people could live on that wage. For that matter, we'd like to know if a denarion provided sufficiency for even just one worker.

A second lesson likewise applies to reading any kind of literature: when looking at a passage from a larger work, we must look around at the broader literary context. This principle applies in a particular way for the parables. Each Gospel has its own way of dealing with the parables.

We begin with Mark. Mark emphasizes that Jesus taught in parables, but he doesn't actually include many when compared to Matthew or Luke. Mark's parables cluster in chapter 4, with one significant parable in chapter 12. Mark's first parable is the Gospel's most extended one, if we count the explanation attached to it. The Parable of the Sower, like the one about the Wicked Tenants in 12:1-12, is an allegory, although Mark's other parables are not. Both parables cut like a knife. Between the Parable of the Sower and its interpretation, Jesus explains to his disciples that parables *prevent outsiders from understanding*. And after Jesus concludes the Parable of the Tenant Farmers, Mark informs us that Jesus directed this parable *against his opponents* (12:12; see 11:27). Both parables cause readers to consider how various people respond to God's word and how God's message gets out to the world—they also function as weapons.

Matthew uses parables differently. Matthew relies heavily on literary context to guide our interpretation. In the verse immediately preceding the Parable of the Workers, Jesus declares, "But many who are first will be last. And many who are last will be first." First and last, last and first. As the parable concludes, Jesus repeats himself, but with a twist, "So those who are last will be first. And those who are first will be last" (20:16). Last and first, first and last. Perhaps, then, we should emphasize the middle of the parable, which just happens to be the hardest part of it for us to understand: at the end of the day, the vineyard owner instructs his manager to pay the workers in reverse order, "beginning with the last ones hired and moving on finally to the first" (20:8).

Matthew also tends to group together related parables, a technique we also encounter in Luke's parables about things lost and found (15:1-32). Matthew clusters parables with judgment and separation imagery. As we found in our exploration of the parables involving weddings (22:1-14; 25:1-13), Matthew emphasizes final judgment themes more intensely than do the other Gospels. Matthew is particularly fond of "weeping and gnashing of teeth" imagery. Perhaps most surprising, several of Matthew's judgment parables feature an element of surprise. One cannot know in advance whether this is the time to put on a wedding garment or to bring extra oil. In Matthew, goats don't know they're goats (25:31-46). But neither do sheep know they're sheep.

Luke has a tendency to tell us what parables mean, sometimes by adding explanations (18:1, 9) and sometimes by placing parables in suggestive locations. The Parable of the Good Samaritan functions as a sharp retort to the legal expert's question, "Who is my neighbor?" (10:29). The Prodigal enters as parable number three in the series of things lost and found parables, all responding to criticism that Jesus welcomes sinners (15:1-2). Likewise, we meet the Rich Man and Lazarus soon after Luke critiques the Pharisees for loving money too much (16:14-15).

Luke also tends to provide inside views of characters' thoughts, a literary technique called interior monologue. That device occurs in only one of the parables in this study. When the Prodigal

> came to his senses, he said, "How many of my father's hired hands have more than enough food, but I'm starving to death! I will get up and go to my father, and say to him, 'Father, I have sinned against heaven and against you. I no longer deserve to be called your son. Take me on as one of your hired hands.'"
>
> Luke 15:17-19

The younger brother does just that, though the speech is unnecessary. His father was already overjoyed by his return.

Another of Luke's tendencies features prominently in our series. Several of Luke's parables involve crisis, when a person begins in a secure spot only to find himself in desperate straits. That happens to the victim of bandits in the Parable of the Good Samaritan. It happens to the Rich Man who neglects Lazarus. The pattern plays a remarkable role in the Parable of the Prodigal Son. The story quickly introduces the Prodigal's crisis: he is destitute. But when the parable closes, the Prodigal has received an abundant welcome. His Father and Older Brother are the ones outside the party. The parable closes without telling us whether the two reconcile.

The Gospel of John includes no parables, so it receives almost no attention in this study. John's Jesus speaks in cryptic metaphors, which provide more than enough for us to chew on.

There's no avoiding that the authors of Matthew, Mark, and Luke shape the parables in their own distinctive ways. In some cases, we can easily imagine taking a parable out of its context in one of the Gospels and examining it as a literary object with its own integrity. That observation raises the question of how authentically the parables reflect Jesus' teachings. How much of a given parable reflects Jesus' voice, and how much is the voice of the Gospel authors? This study minimizes that problem, but for some readers it's a very important question.

This study suggests a third lesson: look for the "hook," that part of a parable where the story abandons conventional logic and jumps off the rails. Not every parable turns on a hook, but many do. We should also be careful: what I see as a hook might not strike other readers in that way. For example, I suggest it's remarkable when the Sower scatters precious seed on poor soil. Many interpreters regard this detail as ordinary. The Parable of the Workers is strange in multiple ways, but I suggest the parable turns around one strange detail: the workers who work the shortest hours receive their pay first, while the others have to watch. Matthew's wedding parables, the Wedding Party and the Bridesmaids, both surprise us when people find themselves excluded for reasons they may not have anticipated. The Parable of the Good Samaritan jolts our imaginations with its surprising hero; rather, it *would have done so for ancient readers*. The Prodigal does not anticipate his father's warm welcome. We might, but his Older Brother certainly doesn't. And Abraham surprises us when he explains the Rich Man's afterlife suffering: you were rich, and Lazarus wasn't. If that's all there is to it, we readers have some thinking to do.

Being alert for hooks in the parables is important. If many parables abandon the logical flow we would expect, that means the parables are more than just nifty teaching illustrations. A parable's hook challenges us to open our imaginations to the possibility that the things of God are not as we'd expect. Parables with hooks refuse to wrap spiritual lessons in fancy paper and tie them up with a pretty bow. Parables challenge us to look one another in the eye, to explore the mystery of the kingdom together (that's Mark's word; 4:10), and to wrestle with the sacred significance of these stories. Appropriating the tennis cliché, the parables whack the ball onto our side of the court.

Fourth, many of Jesus' parables draw upon images we care about deeply. We care about labor and wages, about helping people in need, about messed-up family dynamics, and about the afterlife. Perhaps the parables deploy such imagery to evoke thought about other issues. If so, some say, we shouldn't invest much energy in grappling with those dimensions of the parable: the parables are not "about" such mundane things. I suspect there's truth in that objection. The parables call us to look through them to other realities.

But I also don't like being told how to read. I especially resist rules that tell us what questions we may not ask and experts who tell us our concerns are unimportant. Jesus *chose* ordinary human activities and realities to evoke our reflection. We can well imagine he knew something about work, compassion, family, and concern for the afterlife. Let's take the Parable of the Workers in the Vineyard as an example. It seems noteworthy that Jesus pictures the reign of God through a world in which everyone receives what they need. With that, the ball's in your court.

Resources for Parable Interpretation

Bailey, Kenneth E. *Poet and Peasant, and Through Peasant Eyes: A Literary-Cultural Approach to the Parables in Luke.* Combined Edition. Grand Rapids: Eerdmans, 1983.

A Protestant missionary to Lebanon reads Luke's parables through Middle Eastern cultural lenses. Although dated, still an essential conversation partner.

Crossan, John Dominic. *The Power of Parable: How Fiction* by *Jesus became Fiction* about *Jesus.* New York: HarperCollins, 2012.

Crossan argues that while Jesus' parables challenged their audiences to re-examine conventional assumptions about God and the world, Matthew, Mark, and Luke all adapted Jesus' parables to their own literary purposes.

Hultgren, Arland J. *The Parables of Jesus: A Commentary.* The Bible in Its World. Grand Rapids: Eerdmans, 2000.

A comprehensive commentary on the parables of Jesus, with a focus on historical context.

Levine, Amy-Jill. *Short Stories by Jesus: The Enigmatic Parables of a Controversial Rabbi.* New York: HarperOne, 2015.

Studies in several of Jesus' most popular parables from the distinctive perspective of a scholar who is both Jewish and feminist. Lively writing. A bestseller.

Snodgrass, Klyne R. *Stories with Intent: A Comprehensive Guide to the Parables of Jesus*. Grand Rapids: Eerdmans, 2008.

Like the subtitle says, a massive research commentary on the parables of Jesus. A gold mine of information.

Notes

Introduction

1. C. H. Dodd, *Parables of the Kingdom* (London: Nisbet, 1935), 16.
2. Homer, *The Iliad*, trans. Robert Fitzgerald (New York: Oxford University Press, 2008), 564-69.

1. Divine Inefficiencies

1. Adam Gopnik, "What Did Jesus Do? Reading and Unreading the Gospels," *The New Yorker*, May 24, 2010, www.newyorker.com/magazine/2010/05/24/what-did-jesus-do.
2. I refer reader-learners to Melchert's book, *Wise Teaching: Biblical Wisdom and Educational Ministry* (Harrisburg, PA: Trinity Press International, 1998), esp. 205–71.
3. Mary Ann Tolbert, *Sowing the Gospel: Mark's World in Literary-Historical Perspective* (Minneapolis: Fortress, 1989).
4. Stephen R. Haynes, *The Last Segregated Hour: The Memphis Kneel-ins and the Campaign for Southern Church Desegregation* (New York: Oxford University Press, 2012), 18.

3. Weddings Gone Awry

1. C. H. Dodd, *Parables of the Kingdom* (London: Nisbet, 1935), 16.
2. Dodd, *Parables of the Kingdom*, 16.

4. Lawyers and Samaritans

1. Clarence Jordan, *The Cotton Patch Version of Luke and Acts: Jesus' Doings and the Happenings* (New York: Association Press, 1969), 46–47.

5. Losing, Finding, Partying

1. Henri Nouwen, *The Return of the Prodigal Son: A Story of Homecoming* (New York: Doubleday, 1992).
2. Hank Williams, "I Saw the Light," MGM Records, 1947.
3. I describe this in more detail in my book, *Sinners: Jesus and His Earliest Followers* (Waco: Baylor University Press, 2009).
4. "Best: Decline of the Golden Boy," BBC News, June 14, 2005, http://news.bbc.co.uk/2/hi/uk_news/4090840.stm.

6. A Reversal of Fortune

1. "A Service of Word and Table I and Introductions to the Other Forms," *The United Methodist Book of Worship* (Nashville: The United Methodist Publishing House, 1992), www.umcdiscipleship.org/resources/a-service-of-word-and-table-i-and-introductions-to-the-other-forms.

Afterword

1. John Dominic Crossan, *A Long Way from Tipperary: What a Former Irish Monk Discovered in His Search for the Truth* (San Francisco: HarperSanFrancisco, 2000), 168.